MICHAEL J.
FOX

OVERCOMING ADVERSITY

MICHAEL J. FOX

Richard Kozar

Introduction by James Scott Brady,
Trustee, the Center to Prevent Handgun Violence
Vice Chairman, the Brain Injury Foundation

Chelsea House Publishers
Philadelphia

CHELSEA HOUSE PUBLISHERS

EDITOR IN CHIEF Stephen Reginald
PRODUCTION MANAGER Pamela Loos
ART DIRECTOR Sara Davis
DIRECTOR OF PHOTOGRAPHY Judy L. Hasday
MANAGING EDITOR James D. Gallagher

Staff for **MICHAEL J. FOX**
ASSOCIATE ART DIRECTOR Takeshi Takahashi
DESIGNER Keith Trego
PICTURE RESEARCHER Marty Levick

The Chelsea House World Wide Web site address is:
www.chelseahouse.com

 3 5 7 9 8 6 4 2

Library of Congress Cataloging-in-Publication Data

Kozar, Richard.
Michael J. Fox / Richard F. Kozar
 p.   cm. — (Overcoming adversity)
Includes bibliographical references and index.
Summary: A biography of the actor who starred in the popular television series,
Family Ties, as well as in a number of motion pictures and who recently announced
that he has Parkinson's disease.

ISBN 0-7910-5425-X (hc) — ISBN 0-7910-5426-8 (pb)
1. Fox, Michael J., 1961–   2. Actors—Canada—Biography—Juvenile
literature. 3. Actors—United States—Biography—Juvenile literature. [1. Fox,
Michael J., 1961–   2. Actors and actresses.] I. Title. II. Series.
PN2308.F69 K69 2000
791.43'028'092—dc21
[B]   99–043943

CONTENTS

OVERCOMING ADVERSITY

TIM ALLEN
comedian/performer

MAYA ANGELOU
author

APOLLO 13 MISSION
astronauts

LANCE ARMSTRONG
professional cyclist

DREW BARRYMORE
actress

JAMES BRADY
gun control activist

DREW CAREY
comedian/performer

JIM CARREY
comedian/performer

BILL CLINTON
U.S. president

TOM CRUISE
actor

MICHAEL J. FOX
actor

WHOOPI GOLDBERG
comedian/performer

EKATERINA GORDEEVA
figure skater

SCOTT HAMILTON
figure skater

JEWEL
singer and poet

JAMES EARL JONES
actor

QUINCY JONES
musician and producer

ABRAHAM LINCOLN
U.S. president

WILLIAM PENN
Pennsylvania's founder

JACKIE ROBINSON
baseball legend

ROSEANNE
entertainer

MONICA SELES
tennis star

SAMMY SOSA
baseball star

DAVE THOMAS
entrepreneur

SHANIA TWAIN
entertainer

ROBIN WILLIAMS
performer

STEVIE WONDER
entertainer

ON FACING ADVERSITY

James Scott Brady

I GUESS IT'S a long way from a Centralia, Illinois, train yard to the George Washington University Hospital Trauma Unit. My dad was a yardmaster for the old Chicago, Burlington & Quincy Railroad. As a child, I used to get to sit in the engineer's lap and imagine what it was like to drive that train. I guess I always have liked being in the "driver's seat."

Years later, however, my interest turned from driving trains to driving campaigns. In 1979, former Texas governor John Connally hired me as a press secretary in his campaign for the American presidency. We lost the Republican primary to a former Hollywood star named Ronald Reagan. But I managed to jump over to the Reagan campaign. When Reagan was elected in 1980, I was "sitting in the catbird seat," as humorist James Thurber would say—poised to be named presidential press secretary. I held that title throughout the eight years of the Reagan administration. But not without one terrible, extended interruption.

It happened barely two months after the Reagan administration took office. I never even heard the shots. On March 30, 1981, my life went blank in an instant. In an attempt to assassinate President Reagan, John Hinckley Jr. armed himself with a "Saturday night special"—a low-quality, $29 pistol—and shot wildly as our presidential entourage exited a Washington hotel. One of the exploding bullets struck me just above the left eye. It shattered into a couple dozen fragments, some of which penetrated my skull and entered my brain.

The next few months of my life were a nightmare of repeated surgery, broken contact with the outside world, and a variety of medical complications. More than once, I was very close to death.

The next few years were filled with frustrating struggles to function with a paralyzed right side, struggles to speak and communicate.

To people who face and defeat daunting obstacles, "ambition" is not becoming wealthy or famous or winning elections or awards. Words like "ambition" and "achievement" and "success" take on very different meanings. The objective is just to live, to wake up every morning. The goals are not lofty; they are very ordinary.

My own heroes are ordinary folks—but they accomplish extraordinary things because they try. My greatest hero is my wife, Sarah. She's accomplished a lot of things in life, but two stand out. The first has been the way she has cared for me and our son since I was shot. A tremendous tragedy and burden was dropped unexpectedly into her life, totally beyond her control and without justification. She could have given up; instead, she focused her energies on preserving our family and returning our lives to normal as much as possible. Week by week, month by month, year by year, she has not reached for the miraculous, just for the normal. Yet in focusing on the normal, she has helped accomplish the miraculous.

Her other most remarkable accomplishment, to me, has been spearheading the effort to keep guns out of the hands of criminals and children in America. Opponents call her a "gun grabber"; I call her a national hero. And I am not alone.

After a seven-year battle, during which Sarah and I worked tirelessly to educate the public about the need for stronger gun laws, the Brady Bill became law in 1993. It was a victory, achieved in the face of tremendous opposition, that now benefits all Americans. From the time the law took effect through fall 1997, background checks had stopped 173,000 criminals and other high-risk purchasers from buying handguns, and the law has helped to reduce illegal gun trafficking.

Sarah was not pursuing fame, or even recognition. She simply started at one point—when our son, Scott, found a loaded handgun on the seat of a pickup truck and, thinking it was a toy, pointed it at Sarah.

Fortunately, no one was hurt. But seeing a gun nearly bring a second tragedy upon our family, Sarah became determined to do whatever she could to prevent senseless death and injury from guns.

Some people think of Sarah as a powerful political force. To me, she's the person who so many times fed me and helped me dress during my long years of recovery.

Overcoming obstacles is part of life, not just for people who are challenged by disabilities, illnesses, or tragedies, but for all people. No matter what the obstacle—fear, disability, prejudice, grief, or a difficulty that isn't likely to "just go away"—we can all work to make this world a better place.

Since the mid-1980s, Michael J. Fox has been one of the most popular comic actors in the United States. When the 37-year-old revealed in November 1998 that he is suffering from Parkinson's disease, his many fans were shocked.

1

PARKINSON'S DISEASE

FOR MUCH OF HIS life, the wisecracking Michael J. Fox lived a Hollywood fantasy. He became an actor at age 15, dropped out of high school his senior year to move to Hollywood, survived there until his first real break came in a television sitcom, and subsequently rocketed to fame and fortune thanks to popular TV shows like *Family Ties* and sucessful movies like *Back to the Future*. A string of roles in hit movies followed; then he married a beautiful actress, settled down to raise a family, and began enjoying the fruits of his incredible success.

But just when it looked like he had the world by the tail, at age 30 Michael confronted a real-life crisis more formidable than any he had faced in front of a camera. It wasn't until seven years later—November 1998—that he publicly revealed this problem: he had been secretly suffering from Parkinson's disease.

His legions of fans were devastated. Parkinson's disease is a progressive degeneration of nerve cells in the area of the brain that controls movement. Normally, the disease strikes its victims when they are in their late 50s to early 60s, but 10 percent of the time it affects much younger adults. There is no known cure for the crippling ailment, which causes victims to tremble and suffer from stiffness in their limbs. As the disease progresses, its victims may become unable to walk, communicate, or care for themselves. In the United States, Parkinson's afflicts one million people, mostly elderly Americans. Among the most well-known victims of Parkinson's disease are former boxing champion Muhammad Ali, country singer Johnny Cash, and U.S. Attorney General Janet Reno.

In 1991, Michael first noticed one of the telltale symptoms of Parkinson's—a twitching in his left pinkie. Even though he was making the movie *Doc Hollywood* when his symptoms appeared, Michael became concerned enough to seek medical advice. He visited a Florida hospital near the movie location and consulted a neurologist. The initial diagnosis? At his age, probably just an injured funny bone, suggested the physician.

However, half a year later the twitching afflicted Michael's entire hand, and stiffness had spread to his arm and shoulder. Now back at home in New York City, he visited a specialist who told him that Parkinson's disease was the cause of his growing tremors.

At first Michael couldn't believe it, especially when several subsequent neurologists initially doubted such a young man could contract the illness. But after each specialist ran tests, the diagnoses were the same: Parkinson's disease. Fox and his family were forced to deal with the bad news; he later said the diagnosis was easier for him to accept than it was for those closest to him, including his mother.

In the 1998 *People* magazine article in which he poured out his soul about his illness, the actor who had made his fortune partly because of his boyish good looks was painfully aware of the twist of fate caused by his Parkinson's. "I love the irony," he said. "I'm perceived as being really young, and yet I have the clinical condition of an old man."

Michael and wife Tracy Pollan arrive at the 1998 Primetime Emmy Awards ceremony. Fox credits his wife with helping him cope with his disease.

Why reveal his secret after years of keeping it from all but family and closest friends? For starters, his symptoms had become harder and harder to disguise. After all, few public figures are more visible—or more hounded by the press—than successful actors. Michael and his wife, actress Tracy Pollan, were being chauffeured to the 1998 Golden Globe Awards when the *Spin City* star suffered a particularly acute bout of classic Parkinson's symptoms, including a trembling left arm and leg that he was helpless to control on his own. Aware that the media and fans were waiting for a glimpse of celebrities as they pulled up to the awards show,

Fox asked his driver to circle the block three times to give his medication a chance to take effect and calm the tremors. "I just couldn't get out of the car and let my arm go, or mumble, or shuffle," he said in the *People* interview.

Then there was an appearance on David Letterman's late-night television show, when Michael sat offstage and prayed for his medicine to once again calm the shaking in his arms before he had to go on. Luckily, it did.

While Michael is at home, he is content to go unmedicated, even though this can trigger stiffness in his wrists or require him to drag his leg across a room rather than walk on it. But doing so in public is another story.

From day one, Michael refused to submit meekly to Parkinson's. But after seven long years, he also concluded that his secret was becoming a burden he no longer cared to bear privately. And, as someone who has had a love-hate relationship with the tabloid press, he wanted to be the one who decided when and where his story broke. "It's not that I had a deep, dark secret," he said. "It was just my thing to deal with. But this box I had put everything into kind of expanded to a point where it's difficult to lug around. What's inside the box isn't inhibiting me. It's the box itself. I think I can help people by talking. I want to help myself and my family."

Helping him cope with Parkinson's is Boston neurologist Dr. Allan Ropper, who advised Michael to undergo brain surgery in March 1998 to attempt to relieve his most serious symptom—shaking spells in his left arm that were so bad "I could mix a margarita in five seconds," Fox joked. The innovative but risky operation, performed by Massachusetts neurosurgeon Bruce Cook, was successful. Ropper says his famous patient, with the help of medication and luck, could lead a productive, relatively normal life for as long as another decade.

But even if that isn't the case (some sufferers end up helplessly bedridden, a scenario Michael doesn't waste time contemplating), the upbeat, Canadian-born TV star intends to enjoy life to the fullest, whether he is in front of the camera or after work with Tracy and his three young children. "I'm not crying 'What a tragedy,' because it's not," he told *People*. "It's a reality, a fact."

Although his success has brought with it enough money to retire tomorrow, Fox vows to work as long as possible in the entertainment business.

And because of his celebrity status, Michael also intends to help raise public awareness about his disease. Thanks solely to his public announcement in 1998, various national Parkinson's foundations have reported hundreds of inquiries from people interested in learning more about the surgery he underwent, as well as other treatments. Most of all, Michael remains absolutely convinced that with additional research, he and other Parkinson's sufferers will live to see a cure within the next decade.

Young Michael J. Fox on the set. When he was 18 years old, Michael left Canada and headed to Hollywood hoping to fashion an acting career.

2

SIZE *ISN'T* EVERYTHING

MICHAEL J. FOX has handled Parkinson's disease better than anyone could expect. But that's not so surprising when you look at his entire life and career, which began in rural Canada. For although he has sported boyish good looks and a comedian's charm since he was a teen, Michael also grew up faced with the kind of hurdle not every youngster and teen can easily overcome: he's short, about five feet four inches tall.

Dozens of articles and books have referred to him as "diminutive," which is simply another word for short, but Michael, who has a fondness for not sugarcoating reality, has laughed at the term. "I'm just a short guy," he said matter-of-factly to biographer Dennis Eichhorn. "That's the way it goes. Dustin Hoffman, Al Pacino, Willie Shoemaker, and I—we're all short guys. It's just a fact of life."

His size is a fact that Fox shares with another successful movie star he has always admired: James Cagney, an energetic actor who over-came his short stature by pouring his heart and soul into every role he played. Michael still cherishes a letter from Cagney, which he later framed. It reads: "All signs point to your being little. That goes for me too. Size doesn't mean a thing."

In our society, a young girl who's short is "cute." Males, on the other hand, are more likely to get bullied. Michael says he survived by making friends quickly, especially with bruisers who didn't mind sticking up for him if things got tense. And what he lacked in height he more than made up for in determination, he once told *TV Guide*. "I only got picked last once" on playground teams, he noted. "And whoever did it regretted that they did. If somebody came up to me and said, 'OK, I don't want the little guy,' he was going to feel like an idiot when it was over."

Michael's ability to make friends came in handy. Because his father was in the Canadian Army, he moved his family wherever and whenever the military ordered. This meant the Fox children were forced to switch schools and fit in with other kids several times in their young lives. By all accounts, Michael handled the transitions just fine. "There are a lot of army brats who are actors," he once told biographer Marsha Daly. "You're in different places all the time, different schools. You either find a way to get attention or become a wallflower."

Far from a wallflower, the "slightly hyper" Michael Andrew Fox was born in Edmonton, Alberta, on June 9, 1961. His father, Bill, who at one time was a horse jockey (a job where being short is a plus), was nearly halfway through a military career that would last 25 years in the Army Signal Corps. Michael is the fourth of five children: Karen, Steve (who Michael says was the real comic at the dinner table), Jacki, and Kelli.

Thanks to the Foxes' military lifestyle, Bill and wife Phyllis shuffled from one base to the next, including stops in Chilliwack, British Columbia, and North Bay, Ontario. But by the time Michael was in fifth grade, his family had settled in Burnaby, a suburb of Vancouver, British Columbia, where he would grow up. Michael had an easygoing, fun-loving personality, as well as a love of

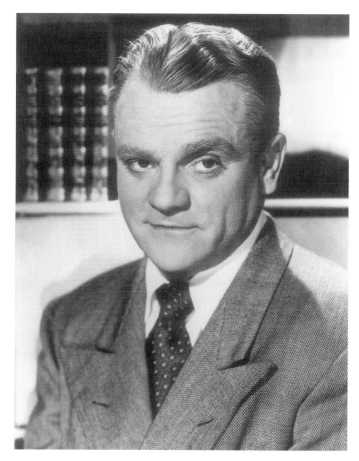

Actor James Cagney was one of Michael Fox's heroes. Like Fox, Cagney is a short actor who became wildly successful. In his long career, which spanned six decades, Cagney played everything from tough gangsters to vaudeville singers and dancers.

sports, that helped him make new friends. He was particularly fond of hockey, which is as beloved in Canada as baseball or football is in the United States. In fact, like many youths north of the border, Michael dreamed of becoming a professional hockey player when he grew up.

Considering his high energy and desire to excel, he might well have made it as a pro—if only his height hadn't stood in the way. Although his speed and agility helped him succeed as a youngster, his fellow hockey players eventually outgrew him when they all became teens. So despite his love of the rugged sport (he is fond of showing off the scars on his body to prove it), the day came in high school when he finally admitted, "I can't do this anymore."

Michael Fox, in his senior year at Burnaby Central High School in British Columbia, Canada. He left the school (pictured at right) in 1979, before graduation.

For some people, the loss of a childhood dream can be devastating. But proving there were more layers to his personality than just a love of sports, Michael began dabbling in drawing and writing, totally different fields that he considered pursuing. He discovered he had a desire to express himself creatively. Michael also was interested in music and learned how to play the guitar. Some of his favorite bands were Bachman Turner Overdrive, Aerosmith, and Led Zeppelin, and he even played some of their music in a small band, just like thousands of other teens all across North America.

About the time Michael was entering Burnaby Central High School, his dad retired from the Army and became a dispatcher with the city's police department. His mother also took a job with an area company. And for the first time, their son was anxious about being so short (at this point only four feet eleven inches). Hoping he would grow taller, he began eating heavily, only to discover he was growing out—swelling to 140 pounds—not up. Looking at Michael now, it's hard to believe that the slim, trim actor ever had a weight problem, but he truly did (and not just in high school).

In high school, Michael became interested in acting in the drama department. "Acting gave me a creative outlet for all my energy," he later explained. In addition, it gave him a medium to act out his fantasies, which ranged from living as an Indian to becoming a rock star.

The truth is, acting was not only something Michael did well, but also a perfect way for a short, otherwise average student to stand in the spotlight. But like most amateur high school actors and actresses, he never once thought he could make a living from acting, let alone become a "star." Few budding actors ever pursue their craft beyond high school musicals and plays.

But Michael's drama teacher, Ross Jones, thought his student had something special going for him: Michael wasn't afraid to throw caution to the wind when onstage,

and he had the burning desire to succeed that separates amateurs from professionals in every field of endeavor. As a favor, the teacher contacted some friends at the Canadian Broadcasting Company and arranged for young Michael to audition for a part in a television show. The role was written for a 10-year-old, but the producers hadn't found anyone who they thought fit the part.

Enter 15-year-old Michael, who for the first time in his life actually found his short stature and youthful appearance a blessing rather than a curse. Who better to play a preteen than a somewhat more mature real teen? Michael landed his first big role on the series, called *Leo and Me*. It was about an Italian con artist who has to be pulled out of jam after jam by his nephew Jamie (Michael). Although *Leo and Me* lasted only 13 weeks, a short run by television standards, it taught Michael a very important lesson—he loved acting, and one way or another, he was going to pursue it as a career.

Canada was a much easier country for a starstruck teen

like Michael to become a young actor. Students there have a great deal more flexibility to work when they are in high school than American youths do. In the United States, the law requires minors (those under 18) to be tutored if they're working outside school. In Canada the laws aren't as tough.

After immersing himself in local theater groups, Michael had another good turn of luck in 1978. The producers of an American television movie being filmed partly in Vancouver agreed to let Michael audition for the role of a grandson to actor Art Carney and actress Maureen Stapleton, both award-winning entertainers. Michael won the part in the movie, called *Letters from Frank*.

Because several scenes in *Letters from Frank* were filmed in Hollywood, Michael was exposed to the heart and soul of the international entertainment industry, which only whetted his appetite to become a full-time actor. In addition, his performance had impressed Carney and Stapleton, who encouraged him to pursue acting in the United States. Best of all, several Hollywood studio executives noticed his performance—people who could open doors for him that didn't even exist in Canada.

Just as hundreds of young theater actors head to New York each year, hoping to make it on Broadway, Michael decided the Los Angeles area was the place to be for an aspiring television and movie performer. Therefore, as he approached his 18th birthday, he debated quitting school altogether, even though he was close to graduating. His mother, quite naturally, wasn't wild about her son's dropping out of school. But his grandmother suggested Michael go for it, confidently predicting he would be famous someday.

So, on his 18th birthday, when he was no longer a minor, Michael packed up his belongings, said goodbye to his family and friends, and drove with his father to Los Angeles. His dad lent him $3,000 and then left him to find his own way. "It was a brave move for me," Michael

Art Carney and Maureen Stapleton were the stars of a television movie called Letters from Frank; *Michael won a small part in the film. The 13 weeks he worked on* Letters from Frank *inspired Michael to move to Hollywood and attempt an acting career.*

observed years later. "But actually, I think I was too innocent to be aware of the risks involved. I just packed my little bags and left."

However, unlike many starving young actors, Michael had a leg up thanks to his work on *Letters from Frank*. A director who worked for Walt Disney Studios thought the Canadian teen would be perfect for a film being made by his company. The title was *Midnight Madness*, and its plot involved teams of college students (jocks, geeks, sorority sisters, and nice guys) who set out on an all-night scavenger hunt in search of treasure. Unfortunately the movie, which was one of Disney's first attempts at attracting teenaged filmgoers by adding adult language and racy situations, was what movie critics call a "dud." It was considered neither funny nor particularly appealing to teens. However, Michael did gain experience from his minor role, as well as a few honorable mentions from entertainment critics.

Meanwhile, during a lull in filming, he had an opportunity to audition for *Ordinary People*, a film about a teenager who is so guilty over the drowning death of his brother that he attempts suicide, undergoes psychiatric counseling, and watches helplessly as his parents' marriage begins to dissolve. Movie superstar Robert Redford, who had been hired to direct the film, was not impressed with Michael's audition. After Michael explained that he had been up all night working on the set of *Midnight Madness*, Redford told him, "Everybody's up all night in Hollywood." Michael didn't get the part.

Michael never forgot the pain of this rejection, saying later, "[Redford] just sat there flossing his teeth during my reading. It was the first time I'd got all pumped up about something and seen it crumble before my eyes." Worse, the role turned out to be an actor's dream come true; Timothy Hutton eventually won an Oscar for his portrayal of the tormented teen.

During *Midnight Madness*, Michael also used his full stage name, Michael J. Fox, for the first time. He decided to change his name in part because another actor named Michael Fox was already registered with the Screen Actors Guild. He also thought going by "Michael A. Fox" (using his real middle initial) might sound a bit egotistical to his fans. He says he instead picked J as his middle initial because he admired the work of Michael J. Pollard, another "diminutive" supporting actor best known as the getaway-car driver in the gangster movie *Bonnie and Clyde*.

Ironically, when Michael retold this story years later on the *Johnny Carson Show*, the other Michael Fox, then working on the soap opera *The Bold and the Beautiful*, saw the interview, in which Michael J. Fox described him as having "played in pictures like *The Brain That Ate Cleveland*." He had never actually worked in that picture, the elder Fox subsequently joked in a letter to Carson, "but if somebody had sent a script, I was undoubtedly available." (The other Michael Fox was still acting in 1996 when he died at age 75.)

Good times continued to roll for young Michael in Los Angeles. No sooner was he done with *Midnight Madness* than he was offered a role in *Palmerstown U.S.A.*, a CBS television series dealing with racial issues in the Depression-era South. Thanks to the two illustrious creators of the show—*All in the Family* producer Norman Lear and Alex Haley, the author of *Roots*—the network expected *Palmerstown* to be a smash, especially since it was filling the slot in which *The Waltons*—a highly acclaimed, warm-hearted family show—had previously aired.

Michael played the part of Willie-Joe Hall, an older brother of a white boy who was friends with a young black lad. For the Canadian-born Fox, becoming a believable Willie-Joe was a challenge because he had to speak with a southern accent. However, despite his hard work and the Lear-Haley pairing, *Palmerstown* lasted only two seasons because it never really caught on with American audiences.

Still, Michael's experience and reputation were growing, as was his bank account. Unfortunately, he also had a tendency to spend money as fast as he made it. But he continued to breeze from one acting job to the next, a real plus for a young actor living in expensive Los Angeles. He appeared as a guest star in such popular 1980s television shows as *Lou Grant*, *Trapper John M.D.*, and *The Love Boat*. Amazingly, Michael had never been out of work since he had packed his bags and left Vancouver. But like all actors, he was about to discover that the entertainment business has both peaks and valleys.

For the first few years of the 1980s, Michael did not have much to smile about. He was struggling to survive in Hollywood when, in 1982, he earned the role that would make him a national success: the character of Alex P. Keaton on the new sitcom Family Ties.

3

TOUGH TIMES IN L.A.

THANKS TO HIS busy acting career, Michael could afford many of the trappings of a single, successful young entertainer, such as fast cars, hip clothes, and a stylish apartment. But his father cautioned him at one point not to get too carried away by his success. "When things are going well, it is like a banquet, and they'll set you down and feed you and entertain you and you'll have a great time," his dad reminded him. "But you have to be aware that at any point, you could become the main course."

That possibility never occurred to his son, who was cruising into another job, this time a smallish role in *Class of 1984*, an independently financed, Toronto-based movie depicting violence unleashed in public schools. It was another attempt to attract teen audiences, and its creators thought the movie could be a critical as well as financial success. The film's plot featured a music teacher's struggles to cope with brutal teen thugs who rule the school's halls and ultimately attack his own family, leading him to seek revenge on his own.

At least one critic had high praise for the movie when it was shown for the first time overseas, but after being released in the United States, *Class of 1984* was trashed by American film reviewers, who generally considered its violence a blatant attempt to exploit young audiences. Some people argued that the picture exaggerated how violent schools actually were in the early 1980s. However, movie fans weren't turned off and came to see the picture in droves, making the film a box-office hit.

One would think Michael's career would continue to surge on the strength of his success to date, but strangely that was not the case. Perhaps it was the added weight he had packed on while filming *Class of 1984*. He had wanted to look bigger for the movie, but once again he had become chubby instead of taller.

Whatever the cause, in the fickle world of Hollywood his rising star suddenly, inexplicably, began to fade. Michael found himself waiting by the phone—but the calls offering television appearances and movies weren't coming in. "My phone suddenly stopped ringing, and I was thirty thousand dollars in debt," he said in a biography.

Soon he had moved out of his luxury apartment and found himself living in a garage apartment in Beverly Hills, eating macaroni and cheese and selling off his beloved car and even his furniture, piece by piece, to make ends meet.

The change in his fortunes aggravated and depressed Michael. After months of living the struggling artist's life for the first time in his career, his mood was so low he seriously considered moving back to Canada and his family. He was still overweight and unemployed. But just as his career seemed on the verge of total collapse, Michael took stock of himself and realized that change was in order, starting with his appearance.

He began by shedding 20 pounds by dieting, noting years later how easy it was because "I couldn't buy food anyway." And then something wonderful happened: he was invited to audition for the part of a teenager in a television comedy called *Family Ties*. Trying out for the role of a high school student seemed like a step backward for someone who had spent the last two years desperately seeking parts for a real-life 20-year-old, but Michael couldn't fathom how important an opportunity *Family Ties* would be for his career.

The funny thing is he almost did not get the part. Competition for the role was fierce. And in his first audition before executive producer Gary Goldberg, who had originally wanted WarGames star Matthew Broderick for the sitcom, Michael made such a poor impression Goldberg ruled him out. Ironically, after reading the script Michael realized he wanted to win the role more than anything he had ever attempted.

Luckily, Goldberg's casting director, Judith Weiner, thought she saw a spark in the boyish-looking actor, so she lobbied hard to give him a second audition. Goldberg relented, and this time took great pains to try to explain to Michael what he thought he was looking for in his character, vaguely describing the part in such a way it was apparent he didn't really know what he wanted Alex P. Keaton to be like.

"Do you know what I mean?" Goldberg asked Michael, following his long-winded explanation. "I have absolutely no idea what you mean," Fox replied, in a tone that was actually closer to Alex's character than either could yet imagine. Nonetheless, the second time around Michael somehow convinced Goldberg that he could play Alex—as a conservative, Brooks Brother's–dressing teen with a sarcastic wit.

"I think I won out by being more obnoxious than the other kids who auditioned," Michael explained in several interviews. "Every time I had gone to a Hollywood audition, I'd seen all of these superfriendly and totally insincere kids dropping names like crazy. I went to the other extreme and put down everyone, which is what the character of Alex was all about. Luckily, it worked."

Now all Goldberg had to do was convince studio executives that a young man could make a mostly teenage
audience believe he really was one of them. At first it was
a tough sell; the network was looking for a beefy male
"hunk" who could help carry the show, someone like John
Travolta of *Welcome Back Kotter*, a hit from a few years
earlier. "NBC asked if [Fox] was the kind of guy you'd put
on a lunch box," Goldberg would later recall. "I'd never
heard of this as a criterion for actors." Making light of the
question, he replied, "Maybe a thermos."

After suffering through a nerve-wracking interview in
front of several dozen NBC executives, with Goldberg
firmly behind him, Michael was relieved to learn
through a phone call to his agent (on a pay phone, no
less; his had been disconnected) that he had finally won
the part. His salary was going to be several thousand
dollars an episode, which struck him as hilarious at the
time because he couldn't afford to buy an inexpensive
bucket of chicken from the fast-food restaurant next to
the phone booth.

Goldberg was convinced audiences would connect
with *Family Ties*. Republican Ronald Reagan, Alex's
idol, was president; the 1980s was the "yuppie" (Young
Urban Professional) decade, and yet the parents of children growing up then were mostly 1960s-era baby
boomers—flower children who had rebelled against
authority, the military, and just about everything else two
decades earlier. Playing the liberal parents Steve and
Elyse Keaton were Michael Gross and Meredith Baxter
Birney, a stunning blond actress with several other television series to her credit. With Alex providing the perfect
contrast to his parents' liberal inclinations, the show
appeared ripe for the generational tension that had made
All in the Family such a hit years earlier for CBS. Except
in *Family Ties*, the children usually would get along far
better with their parents.

The cast of Family Ties, *in the show's first season, included (from left) Michael J. Fox, Michael Gross, Meredith Baxter Birney, Tina Yothers, and Justine Bateman. Michael almost did not get the part; after a poor audition, a casting agent insisted that producer Gary Goldberg give Michael another opportunity. This time, the Canadian actor impressed Goldberg, and he was given the part of Alex.*

Actress Justine Bateman was hired to play Alex's pretty but slightly scatterbrained sister, Mallory, and Tina Yothers won the role of the youngest Keaton, Jennifer. The show was supposed to revolve around Steven and Elyse's characters, with the children as supporting cast, but that's not exactly how *Family Ties* evolved. By the end of the first season, critics and certain television viewers—particularly starry-eyed female teens—had fallen in love with Alex Keaton, and the show's producers realized they had to give his character greater emphasis, with Steve and Elyse taking on the supporting roles.

And despite poor ratings for NBC's entire line-up of half-hour sitcoms (situation comedies) that season—which also included *Cheers,* a show featuring a Boston bar and its patrons—the network wisely decided to keep the shows in its programming, believing that a wider audience would eventually appreciate the warmth and gentle humor in them and begin to tune in. For several years previously, NBC had finished last behind ABC and CBS in the television ratings, which measure how many people watch each network. In many respects, NBC had little to lose by sticking with the shows network executives felt were good.

As anyone who has watched *Family Ties* and *Cheers* knows, of course, both series went on to become popular hits, finishing regularly in the top 20 most-watched programs each week. Much of the credit goes to NBC for allowing the shows to find an audience. But an equal share of the praise for the success of *Family Ties* has to go to Michael, who fleshed out the character of Alex so completely that more than a decade later, many Americans still pictured him as the conservative, suit-and-tie teenager who insisted money was not a dirty word.

Nonetheless, as the popularity of *Family Ties* grew, the suddenly hot young actor frequently went out of his way to praise the contributions of his fellow performers. About Justine Bateman Michael commented, "A lot of people can

Alex lectures his sister Mallory in a scene from the first season of Family Ties. *The warmhearted comedy soon proved to be very popular, and Michael J. Fox emerged as its star.*

act, but she is a real actress." Tina Yothers can "knock you out of a scene," he said. He was equally indebted to Meredith Baxter Birney and Steven Gross, whose on-screen wisdom and maturity provided the perfect balance to his energetic character.

But *TV Guide* critic Robert MacKenzie credited Michael for breathing life into Alex, suggesting the most interesting shows always centered around the materialistic but lovable character, who "doesn't overplay this little gem of a role."

People have often wondered if there is any of Michael

in Alex, but the *Family Ties* star claims that he used his brother Steve as a model for the part. Actually, he told author Dennis Eichhorn, "[Alex and I] are almost complete opposites. Even with his family, Alex is very self-centered. I'm not; my family comes first. I'm a lot less cynical, too. I'm not the kind of political animal Alex is. Also, I'm much more relaxed. I know when it works to make a lot of noise and when it doesn't. I don't think Alex knows that yet." But, he added, "If Alex were more like me, he'd be a lot less fun to play."

Michael has also commented, "I'm like Alex in that I have a sense of right and wrong and I've never dyed my hair blue or engaged in mud wrestling. But I'm an actor, so how conservative can I be?" In addition, he has said, "I think that Alex wouldn't approve of actors. He's such a businessman. He'd probably think acting was a silly way to make money."

If that's the case, Alex would be dead wrong. Michael's career took off again like a skyrocket thanks to *Family Ties*, which soon became one of the most popular shows on television. At last his days as a starving actor were suddenly behind him. For Michael, sucess came just in time: he had had his fill of macaroni and cheese, and he was running out of furniture to sit on.

Still, even after money again began rolling in, he didn't want to repeat the mistakes of his initial success. Granted, he moved out of his tiny apartment to a much nicer hangout in a better section of town, and he did buy another car—but it was a Honda Prelude, not a flashy sports car. He also began socking away money in the bank, just in case his career took another nosedive down the road. "I had blown all of my money the first time I was in a TV series," he explained. " I promised myself that since I'd gotten a second chance, I wouldn't make the same mistake twice."

He also realized luck had played a big part in his career's rebirth. Had he not gotten the right phone call when he did, his career and life might have taken a far different route from the one he ended up traveling. "When [success] happened, it happened quickly," he once observed. But "if things hadn't popped up so easily for me, I'd now be a short longshoreman with a bad back."

Michael, during a Family Ties *scene in the Keatons' living room. By the mid-1980s,* Family Ties *was one of the most popular shows on television, and Alex had become something of a teen idol. "One of the neat things about the job is the acknowledgment," Michael would later say of the reaction by teenage female fans. "No one stops a plumber on the street and compliments him on a faucet rehosing."*

4

THE GRIND

BEING IN A SUCCESSFUL television series is in some ways better than starring in a hit movie: you're seen practically each week by millions of viewers, rather than being in the eye of the public for a few weeks out of the year. In addition you're often asked to do promotional spots to keep the series and your image in the public eye. Finally, the very fact your face is so prominent means there's a good chance movie executives may one day invite you to act on the big screen, every television actor's dream.

This was just the kind of lifestyle Michael settled into, thanks to his *Family Ties* role. When he wasn't filming the series, he frequently appeared on other television productions like *Battle of the Network Stars*, periodic shows that pitted actors from ABC, NBC, and CBS in sports competitions such as swimming, running, and obstacle courses. Because of his love for sports, Michael was a natural contestant for such events, and he even ended up winning a few competitions.

Of course such celebrity status doesn't come without a price, as other famous people well know. Certainly the thousands of fan letters he received each week—most from adoring young girls—were a boost to Michael's ego. But all the attention he was beginning to receive made him realize that home audiences were relating to his character, rather than who he was in real life. Such behavior could be as innocent as a group of teenagers calling him "Alex," rather than by his real name, if they spotted him on the street.

But becoming a teen idol also meant fans watched his every move on TV and in public for clues as to how they should act. That initially amounted to a considerable burden for a young actor who really didn't expect his character on-screen and his actions in public to undergo so much scrutiny.

However, Michael soon realized his portrayal of Alex was positively influencing teens, many of whom considered him a role model. So did Gary Goldberg, who worked hard to come up with scripts in which Alex faced and dealt with dilemmas like other American teens, including a substance abuse problem with diet pills in one episode. Even offscreen, Michael once said, "If I get a chance to talk [with kids] about a drug problem, I jump right in."

Many actors who meet with success at a young age become spoiled and get their names in the news as much for what they do offscreen as for what they do onscreen. However, Michael's commitment to *Family Ties* required so much work that he either had too little time to live the wild life in Los Angeles or, when he could find time, was too tired. He once said, "For a famous person, I lead a very dull life. Most of it is work."

And the *Family Ties* connection was leading to other opportunities. Thanks to his newfound fame, in 1983 he was invited by NBC to play roles in made-for-TV movies, starting with a production called *High School U.S.A.* While the show, which featured a collection of hot young NBC actors and actresses as well as former stars from decades earlier, was hardly Emmy Award–winning material, it did pay the bills, Michael realized. Moreover, the

movie provided another bonus for him: meeting actress Nancy McKeon, who played his girlfriend in the production. McKeon, one of the stars of the television series *The Facts of Life*, became his real-life girlfriend, but both young celebrities shied away from the press, preferring to keep their relationship as private as possible.

As it turned out, *High School U.S.A.* did not win any awards, although it did score well in television ratings. Much of the credit was given to Michael, who was now beginning his second season on NBC. With more and more viewers tuning in to watch *Family Ties*, the show jumped in the ratings, becoming one of the top 20 shows on television for the first time.

After the second season of *Family Ties* was under Michael's belt, NBC once again asked its popular new star

The cast of the NBC-TV movie High School U.S.A. *When it aired,* High School U.S.A. *received good ratings. For Michael (second row, third from left), it was notable as he was introduced to Nancy McKeon during the production; she would later become his girlfriend.*

Michael poses with costar Nancy McKeon in a promotional shot for the 1985 television movie Poison Ivy. *The two actors dated for several years.*

to act in another TV movie, called *Poison Ivy.* The title says it all; the production would not offer him the kind of dramatic role he was hoping to sink his teeth into. Instead it was another lightweight comedy about a camp counselor, Dennis Baxter (Michael), who when he wasn't endearing himself to youngsters dumped at Camp Pinewood, spent his time hitting on attractive girls like costar Nancy McKeon, who played the camp nurse. Naturally, by the time the show ended, Dennis's perseverance had paid off, and he won Nancy's affections.

Predictably, some TV critics were unimpressed with

Poison Ivy, describing it as everything from "witless" to "devoid of subtleties." At least one reviewer was more forgiving, pointing out that the movie wasn't trying to be anything more than a spoof of life in a New England summer camp. NBC had the last laugh as far as viewership was concerned; *Poison Ivy* was as highly rated as other network shows competing in its time slot in February 1985. Good production or bad, Michael's presence on the set definitely made a show worth watching for American audiences.

By 1984 Michael was beginning production of his third year of *Family Ties*. Just when he hoped a great new role would come his way, he was offered a script about a teenage werewolf, which was hardly a novel idea. (Michael Landon had played one at the start of his acting career in the 1950s and had gone on to become a successful entertainer.) Michael's first reaction was to throw the script into the trash, but he decided to read it; he found the script wasn't as bad as he had feared. In fact, *Teen Wolf*, although yet another comedy, "turned out to be the kind of film I'd hoped it would be," he said, "a gentle, funny movie about growing up and knowing who you are."

In many ways, in 1984 Michael was at the top of his game. He was starring in a hit TV show which, thanks to its Thursday-night slot following NBC's wildly successful *Cosby Show*, was beginning to consistently finish number two in the ratings—right behind Bill Cosby's family comedy. In addition, he was making a reported $10,000 an episode for appearing on *Family Ties*, which ensured that his forced diet of macaroni and cheese remained a distant memory.

And thanks to clever planning by NBC executives, Michael and his fellow comedy actors would continue to profit from *Family Ties* even if the show was eventually canceled, thanks to what's known as syndication. This is a process by which major networks sell the broadcast rights to hit shows like *Family Ties*, *Frazier*, and *The Simpsons* to smaller cable networks around the country, which typically rerun the shows five days a week, often year-round. The cable stations don't have to pay to produce the series, thus giving them a relatively inexpensive, sure way to attract steady viewers and advertisers.

As the 1983–84 season of *Family Ties* came to a close, *TV Guide* decided to do a story about Michael, who at 22 had become a teen idol credited with making the series a hit. The reporter attended the taping of the final episode of the season. By 10 o'clock that night, the cast and crew of the sitcom were weary; they had been rehearsing, filming before a live Hollywood audience, and redoing scenes since noon. The only one with a spark of energy, the *TV Guide* reporter noted, was Michael, who seemed to rejuvenate those around him just by bounding back onto the stage for a final shot. Michael's enthusiasm and energy livened up the crowd, and everyone focused long enough to complete episode 46.

Afterward a season-ending party was planned, but most of the cast and crew were too beat to really whoop it up during the celebration. The one exception was Michael, who worked the crowded set like Bill Clinton running for election. "The boy just zaps through life," marveled his TV mother, Meredith Baxter Birney.

Perhaps, but the grind of working on a hit sitcom took its toll on the young actor, who was such a hot commodity that he couldn't walk into a pizza shop without drawing admiring stares from young ladies. Once, after his debut season on the show, he was startled on his first trip to New York City to hear a nearly hysterical female fan shout, "Marry me!" Michael later said, "I mean, every actor likes to have visible evidence that his work is affecting people—but this was truly ridiculous."

Then there were the two days of interviews, 36 in all, he had just completed thanks to being the star of a top-five television show. While the journalists no doubt struggled to ask him questions he had never before been asked (a seemingly impossible task), Michael felt like 36 times he he had to discuss "how I am not like Alex Keaton" and tell reporters over and over that he was "not overwhelmed being a teen-age idol." Joking with one reporter, Michael mockingly asked himself a trite interview question— "What are your goals?"—then responded, "Women, money and world domination."

Such is the life of a rising star, especially one in constant demand. Michael, even at this young age, was finally beginning to accept this fact. But fame and success can only bring so much happiness, he began to hint to his many interviewers. After three years in a successful series, his performance as Alex Keaton was becoming somewhat predictable. "He's kind of like a shirt that I can put on and take off," Michael told one writer.

The implication was that he was once again yearning to spread his creative "wings," hoping for the role that might, if not earn him an Oscar, at least allow him to play a character who would not be restricted to Alex Keaton's familiar personality. He couldn't help being slightly envious of his peers who had made names for themselves in motion pictures that were critically acclaimed and even box-office successes.

Little did Michael know that in the following year, he would play a character not only more carefree than Alex, but one he could exploit financially far, far into the future.

Michael gets to show off one of his loves—playing the guitar—in this scene from Back to the Future. *The humorous film became one of the highest-grossing movies of all time, and catapulted Michael to superstardom.*

5

TIMING IS EVERYTHING

AT SOME POINT, all successful actors can look back at a point when they got the role that sent their careers skyward, either thanks to hard work, great performances, or just plain luck. The trouble is, not all performers recognize the "big break" when it's in front of them. It's only after taking—or passing up—a role, that they can look back and safely say "Yep, that was my big break. I'm glad I seized it!" (or, "sorry I missed it!")

How can entertainers not know opportunity when it comes knocking? Well, not every television show or feature-length movie looks as good on paper as it might turn out on the screen. Take *Star Wars*. The first movie in the now-famous series starred actors who were virtual unknowns outside of the entertainment industry in 1977: Harrison Ford, Mark Hamill, and Carrie Fisher. On paper the movie sounded like just another run-of-the-mill sci-fi flick. But thanks to director George Lucas's mind-boggling special effects and an exciting story line, all three actors gained fame and fortune. In Ford's case, the role of Han Solo in *Star Wars* was just the beginning of a fabulously successful acting career.

Even Michael J. Fox, who has a finely tuned sense of comic timing that some have compared to the late Jack Benny's, almost blew his chance at the movie role that changed his career. It was 1985, and he was working on year four of *Family Ties*. The show's producer, Gary Goldberg, heard that Steven Spielberg was looking for a young male actor to replace Eric Stoltz, who had won the lead role for Spielberg's current movie but wasn't working out. The film, which Spielberg was producing, was called *Back to the Future*. Gossip had it that Stoltz, although a successful dramatic actor who had won rave reviews for his performance of a disfigured teen in *Mask*, just wasn't delivering the kind of energetic performance Spielberg was looking for in the science fiction adventure flick. There were also rumors that he was being "difficult."

Word on the street was that Spielberg, a Hollywood giant who had directed such hits as *Jaws*, *Raiders of the Lost Ark*, and *E.T.*, had always wanted Michael to play the part of Marty McFly, a teenager who ends up transported back in time to the 1950s, when his own parents were just on the verge of dating. Michael had turned down the role months before because he was committed to *Family Ties*. But now Spielberg approached Gary Goldberg, hopeful that the *Family Ties* producer could convince his young star to work on the movie after all.

The second time around, Michael still balked at doing the movie. "No way," he recalled saying at the time. "They've already got a guy. I don't want to do it." The *Family Ties* actor wasn't anxious to step into a production that had already been filming for six weeks, fearing the final product would be a mishmash. However, Goldberg insisted that Spielberg was willing to eat the million-dollar costs of starting filming all over again if Michael was willing to sign on. Moreover, Goldberg told Michael that he did not have a problem if the young actor worked on the television show and feature film simultaneously.

Considering Spielberg's influence in Hollywood, it's no

Christopher Lloyd (right) played a wacky doctor who invents a time machine in Back to the Future, *while Michael portrayed a high-school student who has befriended the madcap inventor and is accidentally sent back in time 30 years, to 1955.*

wonder Michael eventually caved in and agreed to work on *Back to the Future*. After all, how often does one of Hollywood's most influential producer-directors beg an actor to be in his movie? Michael had no sooner signed the contract than he was handed a script and told to show up for filming five days later. He had no idea how grueling a schedule he would have to keep for the next several months, when his life would truly consist of little more than work.

Each day Michael shot scenes for *Family Ties* from 10 A.M. to 6 P.M. But just when his fellow performers were heading home for dinner and a relaxing evening, he was hustled over to the movie set of *Back to the Future*, where rehearsals and shooting began a half hour later and didn't wrap up until 2:30 A.M. During this hectic schedule, one day blurred into the next. But afterward Michael was philosophical about the drain on his mind and body. "I had to learn to enjoy it," he recalled. "Besides, if I couldn't handle the pace at my age, I figured I might as well get out of the business. I averaged about four hours of sleep a night. Energy was in very short supply at the time. . . . It was just one of those things. Working such long hours really taxes your sanity. But what was I going to do? The movie had to get done."

Michael remembered he was roused out of sleep each morning by a studio chauffeur who alternated between throwing him in the shower to wake him up and tucking him into bed each night to ensure he got at least a few hours of rest. One of the toughest challenges he faced was keeping straight which personality he was supposed to portray at which time. For example, while Alex was a straight-laced conservative fond of starched shirts and ties, Marty was a carefree adventurer who tooled around on a skateboard. Compounding matters, Marty was also a high-energy character who had to think on the fly in *Back to the Future*. "They wanted Marty to have some of the same qualities that Alex had. They wanted that energy and that

Michael had filmed Teen Wolf *before making* Back to the Future*; however, the film did not come out until just after* Back to the Future *had already become a big hit.* Teen Wolf *was nowhere near as spectacular as* Future*, but Michael's presence propelled it to very good ticket sales.*

same crazy character," Michael said. However, he added, "It became very tough. I found myself dealing with three personalities, and mine got the worst of it."

Furthermore, many people were skeptical Michael could manage the pace of what amounted to two full-time jobs requiring him not only to show up for work but also to act like he was having fun. He quickly eased everyone's anxieties, however, proving he was up to the task physically and theatrically. The grueling, 18-hour days lasted Monday through Friday for two full months, at which point even he admits his batteries were nearly drained.

"About two weeks before I finally finished *Family Ties*, my brain seriously started to turn to cheese, but I just kept going," he said.

With good reason. Most people on the set of *Back to the Future*, particularly producer Spielberg and the movie's director, Robert Zemeckis, were becoming convinced the movie had the makings of a hit. Spielberg likened it to "the greatest *Leave It to Beaver* episode ever produced." And what these two moguls thought meant a great deal in Hollywood, where money and power gravitate to those who can consistently come up with creative and financial hits. Their main mission was to finish filming in time for a summer release, when they counted on millions of American teens lining up at movie theaters across the country to see their movie.

The plot was certainly novel: With the help of Doc (zany Christopher Lloyd), 17-year-old Marty is accidentally sent back in time in a souped-up Delorean, a stainless-steel car that, thanks to a plutonium-charged engine, propels Marty back to 1955. He appears in his hometown, Hill Valley, where he bumps into his future mother and father, who are high school students. Unfortunately, his mother (Lea Thompson) develops a crush on *Marty*, rather than falling in love with his future dad (Crispin Glover). Marty must get his parents together; otherwise, he will cease to exist in the future.

Michael was required to perform some hair-raising stunts and initially had a little trouble getting used to the special effects–laden set, but he persevered. He especially enjoyed playing guitar in a big high school dance scene— he introduced the crowd to rock 'n' roll music. Even he was beginning to wonder if *Back to the Future* could be the movie that would propel him to the big time. It certainly had a bigger budget, a more interesting plot, and greater expectations than any of his previous projects.

Despite several other movies competing with *Back to the Future* for ticket buyers, the movie opened big on the

Fourth of July in 1985, and just got bigger. It was number one at the box office for weeks, eventually earning the studio over $300 million dollars worldwide, an astounding figure in those days. In addition, it earned genuinely favorable reviews. Critic Chad Polenz gave it four out of four stars, gushing that it was "one of the greatest modern films. The adventure, the excitement, and the total creativity are all so original and so well assembled there is not one point in the movie where you would remotely lose interest or become skeptical." He added, "Movies that are this much fun with such innocence are really a unique phenomenon."

Michael J. Fox and Nancy McKeon visited the White House in October 1985, where they had dinner with President Ronald Reagan and his wife, Nancy.

Newsweek's Jack Kroll called *Back to the Future* "the smartest, sweetest, funniest comedy in many summers," while well-known movie critic Gene Siskel especially liked the plot twist where Marty has to make certain his parents fall for each other (and ensure Mom doesn't fall for him). Siskel further predicted that, based on his portrayal of Marty, Michael should have little difficulty getting more parts in feature films.

As if Michael weren't already on a roll, the makers of *Teen Wolf* cleverly decided to release their film on the heels of *Back to the Future*. Although this movie was hardly the same quality as *Back to the Future*, thanks to Michael's sudden popularity it drew viewers in droves and earned $33 million. In fact, the flicks were number one and two at the box office for several weeks in the summer of 1985.

In *Teen Wolf* Michael plays another teenager, one with an unusual cosmetic talent: he can turn into a wolf on a whim. However, unlike Michael Landon and countless other actors who have played werewolves as tormented demons, Michael played a wolf boy that doesn't maul anybody. Instead, he manages to turn his losing basketball team's fortunes around, mostly by distracting opposing players with his furry "uniform." On top of that, he finds that his new look makes him stand out in a crowd. No wonder Michael had decided to make this movie a year earlier.

But after those lean years of struggling for any acting jobs, he had difficulty imagining how he could deliver such a one-two punch at the box office. Instead, he always just tried to do the best acting job that he could. "I never really thought about how much appeal the film would have or how much money it would make," he said shortly after *Back to the Future* became a phenomenon. "If I had, I wouldn't have been able to do my job, which is to concentrate on what I'm doing."

By August 1985, Michael was basking in the glow of his success and trying to catch his breath from several years of nonstop activity. It still hadn't ceased; he was in

Numerous awards were presented to Michael in 1985, including the Hollywood Radio and Television Society's Man of the Year in Broadcasting.

England after agreeing to yet another made-for-NBC TV movie, this time about a subject dear to his heart—*Family Ties (on) Vacation*. Although some observers wondered if, like many television actors before him, he would stick to the big screen from now on, Michael let it be known he hadn't forgotten how he became successful in the first place. "I can't turn my back on *Family Ties* now," he said. "In fact, I could stay with it forever. I like the show, I like the people, I like the security, and I love the character." Besides, he noted in a *Maclean's* interview, becoming a movie star has its perils. "Doing television, you get recognized in a certain way. But when you have a film, people want to take bits of your body home with them."

Of course, he was learning that being a full-fledged movie star had its perks as well. Because of his busy schedule, Michael hadn't even seen *Back to the Future* while he was in London. So the first thing he did after returning to Los Angeles was mention that fact to his local theater—which promptly invited him to see it "on the house." And instead of pulling up into a parking space reserved for the occasion in his Honda Prelude, he showed up in in a far sportier new Datsun 300 ZX. Michael also bought a three-bedroom home in Laurel Canyon, a desirable section of Los Angeles. It had fireplaces, hardwood floors, a swimming pool, and a spa. And why not splurge a little? After all, Michael was pulling down $15,000 an episode for *Family Ties*, now entering its fourth season and being watched by an estimated 60 million viewers each week.

Indeed, Michael J. Fox was in demand like never before. There was a visit to the White House, where he met President Ronald Reagan and Princess Diana of England. He was selected as Most Exciting New Star of 1985 by the National Association of Theater Owners, Movie Star of the Year by the readers of *16* magazine, and even one of America's ten best-dressed men, by the national Hairdressers and Cosmetologists Association.

And then there were all those fan letters—21,000 a week, the most any NBC star was receiving. "I never get tired of getting letters from people who like my work," he said at the time. But unless he wore his traditional baseball cap and sunglasses to shield his identity, he would quickly be surrounded by autograph hounds the minute he stepped out in public. However, his popularity made him realize he had a strange power to do good for others. "You can blow some kid away by doing nothing, just by talking and saying 'How are you? Nice bike you got there. I used to have one like it when I was a kid,'" he told an interviewer.

The highlight of 1985 may have been October 24, when Michael stood in for ailing star James Cagney, who had been invited to speak about his coming of age as an Irish-American at a fund-raiser for the Statue of Liberty renovation. The "diminutive" but charismatic Cagney, who had played everything from pushy gangsters to vaudeville singers and dancers, had always admired Michael and asked him to read his remarks at the fund-raiser. In fact, the Canadian actor was Cagney's personal choice to portray him in any future biographical film.

From his lofty vantage point atop the entertainment industry, the only question Michael had to ask himself now was, what should he do for an encore? He once said, "I've got everything I want, but sometimes it's scary to see your ambitions fulfilled so quickly. Where do I go from here?"

Thanks to Michael's success on television—he won the 1986 Emmy Award for his work on Family Ties—*as well as in movies such as* Back to the Future *and* Teen Wolf, *the young actor soon found himself deluged with scripts for big-screen projects.*

6

GOOD TIMES ROLL

THE 1980S CONTINUED to be a wonderful decade for Michael. Thanks to his exposure on *Back to the Future* and *Teen Wolf*, more people than ever were watching *Family Ties*. In 1986 the 25-year-old was nominated for an Emmy, television's highest award, as Best Lead Actor in a Comedy Series. Michael won the coveted Emmy, beating out such heavyweights as Bob Newhart, Ted Danson (*Cheers*), and Harry Anderson (*Night Court*). He had indeed arrived on the entertainment scene.

Movie scripts began pouring in to him, most of which he ignored because virtually all had him playing characters younger than his own age. But one caught his eye: *Born in the U.S.A.*, written by movie director Paul Schrader.

Schrader's past works included several critically acclaimed projects, *Taxi Driver* and *Raging Bull* being the most notable. Critic Roger Ebert called him "one of the most consistently interesting writers and directors" of the 1980s. All of the characters in his dark and brooding scripts, Ebert said, have pasts that "keep them imprisoned, and shut them off from happiness in the present."

In the film Light of Day, *Michael and rock singer Joan Jett played siblings determined to make it big with their Cleveland bar band. Pictured are band members Michael Dolan and Michael McKean, Jett and Fox, and the band's drummer, Paul J. Harkins.*

"I was sitting at home after *Back to the Future* reading scripts about 18-year-old kids who have big adventures when I received the script from Paul Schrader," Michael said. "It was a dream come true. I think he's one of the greatest screenwriters in America."

One thing was certain: the role that Schrader envisioned for him in *Born in the U.S.A.* was unlike any other that Michael had played, and yet it was closer to his own personality than any other. He would be Joe Rasnick, who at age 22 was just a few years younger than Michael's real age. He lived in Cleveland, worked in a factory by day, and played in a rock group called Barbusters each night with his temperamental sister, Patti (rock performer Joan Jett).

The part was appealing because Rasnick was a tough character; this intrigued Michael, who had always hoped to play dramatic roles. It also allowed him to play the guitar—one of his favorite pasttimes—throughout the film, something he had only had a chance to do in one scene in *Back to the Future*. "It was a great opportunity," said Michael. Rasnick was also a tougher character, which intrigued Michael, who had always hoped to play dramatic roles. Paul Schrader called Michael a "likable actor, but he doesn't have to be so clean-scrubbed."

What made the script much different from anything Michael had done lately was the tension between Joe, Patti, and their mother and father, who were average working-class parents who had managed to afford a home and raise children. But sparks flew between Patti and her mother; mom (Gena Rowlands) used religion to lay a guilt trip on her daughter, whom she felt was headed down the road to destruction. Patti felt rock 'n' roll was the most important thing in the world, even more so than her illegitimate young son, whom she dragged from one seedy hotel to another when the band toured.

Meanwhile, Joe was continually trying to make peace, taking on the impossible task of keeping everyone happy, while his mild-mannered father stood hopelessly by. Things got really emotional when Gena Rowlands' character became sick and used her maternal influence to make things turn out the way she wanted.

Like many movie projects in Hollywood, *Born in the U.S.A.* didn't quite end up the way it was first envisioned. For one thing, the title changed after singer-songwriter Bruce Springsteen, who had been sent a copy of the script, asked Schrader if he could name his new album *Born in the U.S.A.* In return, Springsteen agreed to write another song for the movie, both of which were eventually called *Light of Day*.

The film was shot on location in the gritty cities of Cleveland and Chicago to make it more realistic. In addition, Joan and Michael switched professions somewhat before production began; he took guitar lessons to make his playing sound more professional, while she worked with an acting coach to make her character more believable on screen. Michael told Joan, "I'll take you seriously as an actor if you take me seriously as a musician."

Michael's starring role in *Light of Day* proved he was a valuable commodity; now all the big hitters in Hollywood were trying to cash in on his success. "The minute we had him, we had just about every studio in town calling," said producer Rob Cohen.

Light of Day turned out to be modestly successful, but not the incredible smash that *Back to the Future* had been. If anything, the Springsteen song and its accompanying made-for-TV video, in which both Michael and Joan appeared, were bigger hits.

Movie offers continued to roll in. His next film was initially called *Private Affairs*, but the title ultimately became *The Secret of My Success*. In it, Michael plays Brantley Foster, a farm boy from Kansas who wants to make it big-time in New York City. His business-executive uncle arranges a job for him—in the mailroom. But thanks to an opportunity that falls into Brantley's lap, he begins leading a double life in the company, both as mailboy and as a mysterious management-level executive. Within a few weeks, he ends up in the company boardroom fighting for control of the whole place. Along the way, Brantley is nearly seduced by the wife of the company's president (who happens to be his aunt), and he woos and wins a fellow corporate executive, played by Helen Slater (who would later be romantically linked to Michael in the Hollywood tabloids).

The *Secret of My Success* was like Michael's previous roles before *Light of Day*; a lightweight comedy where Michael's character ultimately wins out thanks to his charm and perseverance. "In Brantley, I hoped everyone would see a bit of the hustler in themselves, and I hoped they would also see the way he could laugh at himself," Michael said.

The Secret of My Success was popular with movie fans—another success on his film résumé. And he kept right on working, beginning with the fifth season of *Family Ties*, in which he and Gary Goldberg took the opportunity

to stretch the role of Alex in new and different directions. In one classic episode, for instance, Alex has to come to terms with the death of Greg, one of his best friends. If ever there was a chance for an actor to send a message to his teenage viewers, this was it. "When I got the part of Alex, I was really easygoing about the part," Michael would later tell reporters. "But when I realized Alex was a role model, I started putting more into the character. I continue to do that today."

Alex was so deliciously easy to write for because, like other memorable television characters, people could almost predict how he would react in a given situation. Almost, that is. In another unusual *Family Ties* episode, called "Gandhi and Gidget," Alex finds himself confronted with a second character-shaping event.

It all starts innocently enough, with Alex and Jennifer bantering about his having to take a humanities course in college, which is about the last thing the business-minded

An anxious moment for Brantley Foster (Michael), who is being seduced by the rich wife of a powerful executive in the company he works for. The moment becomes even more stressful for Brantley—and more humorous for the audience— when he realizes that the seducer is actually his aunt.

young man wants to waste his time on.

> ALEX: Well, the choices are absurd. Listen to this one,
> Humanities 1: Man, society, civilization, and the
> universe. How am I supposed to relate to this stuff?

> JENNIFER: Just don't talk in class, and they'll think
> you're one of them.

> ALEX: Jennifer, I'm in college to learn about money, not
> people.

> JENNIFER: Alex, there's more to life than just getting
> rich. People who need people are the luckiest people
> in the world.

> ALEX: Jennifer, people who have money don't need
> people.

Eventually, Alex, an economics major, opts to work at a campus counseling hotline, where students are trained to talk callers through their personal problems. All Alex cares about is that he get credit for a humanities course—and use the time there to "catch up on my real courses."

He finds himself working the first night with James Jarret, a former high school rival who is now attending the same college as a psychology major. Because the counseling hotline has a rule that its phone operators must choose code names, Alex picks the name "Gandhi," without explaining why. In the heat of a tense call, James settles on the name "Gidget."

The episode takes a dramatic turn when a caller named Bill tells Alex, "I need some help here. I think I'm gonna' kill myself." Alex puts him on hold and tries to transfer him to James. Both then listen to the caller, who tells them, "You know, I spent all last week trying to think of one good reason to live, and I couldn't do it."

Before long, Alex and James accidentally hang up on Bill, who finally calls back, saying, "Is that how you help? A guy says he's gonna kill himself and you hang up on him?" Alex and James try reading from the hotline manual, but Bill rejects its textbook advice.

BILL: Guys, I appreciate what you're doing, but you're just wasting your time. Nobody cares about me.

ALEX: Hey, we do. And we're gonna stay on this phone as long as you want us to.

BILL: Come on, you're just two guys who work at the hotline and happened to show up on the wrong night. I don't even know your real names.

When Alex and James tell the caller their names, Bill says, "I didn't think you'd tell me. Isn't that against the rules?"

ALEX: Bill, at a time like this, everything goes out the window. . . . Let me rephrase that.

BILL: Look, I know you guys are really trying, but you still haven't told me why I should keep living.

JAMES: Think of good things. Think of falling snow. Think of falling in love.

BILL: I know, every cloud has a silver lining.

ALEX: No, silver's down this week. Say every cloud has a zinc lining. (Bill laughs.)

Finally, Alex confesses to being scared himself at times, especially when he worries about the future and whether he might fail at something. Bill can relate, telling the two he wants to go to bed now and start thinking about how to straighten out his life.

JAMES: Nice going Keaton. You're really something man.

ALEX: You're not so bad yourself. (They hug.)

ALEX: Listen, about all that stuff about being scared and all.

JAMES: Yeah?

ALEX: Well, you know I was just saying that.

JAMES: Oh yeah, I know you don't get scared. (James turns off the lights to leave.)

ALEX: Uh, James, can you leave the light on?

In a two-part Family Ties *episode from 1985, Alex kisses a girl named Ellen (played by Tracy Pollan), whom he has fallen in love with, to stop her from leaving town to marry another man. A few years later, Michael and Tracy would find they had feelings for each other beyond those of their on-screen characters.*

7

REAL FAMILY TIES

DESPITE HIS DENIALS, Michael might have been more like Alex in some respects than he ever wanted to admit. In the "Gidget and Gandhi" *Family Ties* episode, Alex Keaton revealed that he often stays awake nights worrying about failing someday, and wondering how he'd deal with not being the best and brightest. Although Michael has never come out and made a similar statement, his driven approach to acting and work is reminiscent of a shark afraid that if it stops swimming, it'll sink. Even after the runaway success of *Back to the Future*, Michael continued to live his life as if he still had something to prove.

For the time being, that wasn't the case with *Family Ties*, which ended 1986 as the second-most-watched show in the ratings behind the *Cosby Show* and earned Michael his second Emmy a year later. However, by 1987 the show had been bumped from its dream Thursday-night slot behind *Cosby* and moved to Sunday nights, where it was up against *Murder She Wrote*, a very strong CBS television series starring Angela Lansbury. Although Michael would earn yet another Emmy for his now-familiar portrayal of Alex Keaton, *Family Ties* closed out the

Kiefer Sutherland and Phoebe Cates starred with Michael in the film version of Jay McInerney's Bright Lights, Big City. *Michael is Jamie Conway, a would-be writer with a boring job as a fact checker at a prestigious magazine; Cates plays his wife, a model who leaves him as her career takes off. Sutherland plays Tad Allgash, who plies Jamie with booze and drugs until he finally reaches a breaking point.*

1988 season 17th in the ratings.

In his movie career, Michael continued choosing roles about as far as possible from Alex Keaton's character. From all appearances, he seemed intent on becoming a "serious" actor. *Bright Lights, Big City*, based on a best-selling novel by Jay McInerney, was his next attempt. Released in 1988, the film stars Michael as Jamie Conway, a twenty-something New Yorker who works as a fact-checker for a prominent magazine. His dull job is just a way to pay his bills, however, and support the cocaine addiction around which his entire life revolves. Jamie stumbles through work, not caring whether he's doing a passable job or not. By night his only consolation is alternating between the numbness of alcohol and cocaine. *Bright Lights, Big City* shows Jamie's downward spiral into drug addiction as he wonders when he will hit bottom.

Michael earned good reviews for his performance of

Jamie, particularly from critic Roger Ebert, who said, "Fox is very good in the central role (he has a long drunken monologue that is the best thing he has ever done in a movie). To his credit, he never seems to be having fun as he journeys through club land." Michael's fans were not as impressed with his latest portrayal, however, and relatively few bothered to indulge their curiosity at theaters. *Bright Lights, Big City*, just like *Light of Day*, was a disappointment at the box office.

For Michael, one of the highlights of making *Bright Lights, Big City* was the opportunity to work again with Tracy Pollan. An attractive blond actress, Tracy had also appeared as Alex Keaton's occasional love interest on *Family Ties* in 1985. She is almost a year to the day older than Michael, and grew up in Long Island, New York. Tracy has played in several feature films, including *Baby, It's You* (1983), as well as numerous made-for-TV movies.

Although there were rumors from her first appearance on *Family Ties* that Tracy and Michael also had an off-screen romance, Michael has always claimed that wasn't the case. He was, after all, something of a steady beau to actress Nancy McKeon. Meanwhile, Tracy had been living with actor Kevin Bacon for several years. "I always thought she was cool, but it was like a couple of married people who worked together and liked each other," Michael told *People* years later.

But after *Bright Lights, Big City*, he suddenly saw Tracy, who was now unattached, in a whole new light, and they quickly began dating. Their courtship lasted 14 months, and he proposed on December 26, 1987. "The toughest part was trying to figure out when to get married, and then to figure out how nobody else could know about it," Michael said. While news of any Hollywood marriage attracts tabloids like hounds to a fox, Michael and Tracy's proposed nuptials merited special scrutiny because the two were young, popular, and most of all, determined that their marriage be a private affair.

Little did the couple know just how difficult that last wish would be to pull off. Michael was so astounded over the increasing pressures the media was putting on celebrities that he decided to write a lengthy magazine article for *Esquire* about the wedding preparations with the help of Tracy's brother, Michael, executive editor of *Harper's* magazine. It amounted to an insider's view of the lengths that celebrities must go to for privacy—and the incredible lengths the tabloid media would go to invade that privacy.

Rumors swirled in entertainment circles that the two planned to tie the knot at Michael's new 120-acre farm in South Woodstock, Vermont; at Tracy's parents' rural home in New York; or at *Family Ties* producer Gary Goldberg's New York residence. But Michael and Tracy secretly (they thought!) decided to hold the wedding ceremony at a remote inn in Vermont, far from the probing cameras of the Hollywood press. They thought that by swearing the inn owners to secrecy and telling a local florist that Tracy's sister was actually the bride they could keep the press in the dark. However, a glaring story in a supermarket tabloid about threats on Tracy's life all but assured intense media coverage of their every appearance, so Michael hired Gavin de Becker, a Hollywood guardian to the rich and famous, as a consultant.

De Becker told the couple there was only "one chance in a million" they could keep the festivities a quiet, family affair, especially with so many wedding guests traveling to scenic Vermont. Why? Because de Becker estimated that the bigger tabloids could easily fork over $150,000 for a wedding shot of the famous couple; that's how much their sales would surge in grocery stores throughout America with an exclusive cover photo of the ceremony.

Before long, Michael and Tracy's worst fears started to come true. Rumors of their pending wedding leaked, and reporters even began calling family members to confirm the event. Moreover, sensing a scoop, several publications offered the two money or favorable publicity in exchange for exclusive wedding coverage. Michael and Tracy declined all these offers.

As the July 16 wedding date neared, however, it became clear the entertainment press (which already knew the date) would bend over backwards to pin down the location of the event. Reporters acting as tourists—and even family members—began showing up at the inn asking the staff all sorts of personal questions. Members of the tabloid press knew from firsthand experience that some people love to let others in on a secret. And if that doesn't work, a $100 bill sometimes does.

For security purposes, Gavin de Becker meticulously scoped out the inn and surrounding countryside. He had even presented the *Family Ties* star with a 36-page itinerary for the wedding, outlining security checkpoints, event times and places, and even code names (Michael and Tracy were Coyote One and Two). It all seemed like a bad spy novel, Michael thought.

But de Becker knew better. As the wedding drew near, one cunning reporter had nearly convinced Tracy's trusting but elderly grandparents to take a sightseeing tour of Vermont with him—during which, naturally, he would pump them for details of the ceremony. Suspicious family members intervened just in time.

Next, acting on a tip that one tabloid was setting up a command post at a nearby hotel, Michael's publicist, Nancy Ryder, agreed to apply for a temporary position with the paper's reporter to learn what they were up to. The man hired Nancy without realizing that he had been hounding her for the past week by phone to cut a deal with his publication for an exclusive story.

Incredibly, Nancy overheard a member of the tabloid staff say they were hiring two helicopters to guarantee continual aerial coverage of the inn and, hopefully, the wedding ceremony. In addition, the tabloid employees had come up with the brilliant idea of disguising a photographer in a llama suit so he could sneak across the inn's rolling pasture and presumably catch the unsuspecting couple in a bridal pose.

Meanwhile, reporters from various papers were promising cash payments to anyone remotely connected with the inn and wedding for access, including one of the inn's bartenders. A local resident, acting on behalf of one of the tabloids, offered one of the inn's barmaids $1,500 for a picture of the Foxes. Before the conversation ended, he had upped the offer to $10,000 without blinking an eye when the woman half-jokingly said she would need at least that much to do such a thing. The bartender ultimately declined to go along with the scheme, but only because her conscience wouldn't permit her to do otherwise.

Just getting to the inn the morning of the wedding without giving the tabloid photographers a free photo turned out to be a production. Michael and Tracy had to be escorted separately down to their waiting car outside a nearby hotel to deprive the *paparazzi* (a name given to freelance celebrity photographers) of a picture going to the wedding. The swarm of photographers followed the car, first on foot and later in a stream of cars with a helicopter trailing overhead. A short jaunt from one inn to the other that normally took less than 10 minutes required nearly 40 thanks to the vehicle congestion on the highway.

And when Michael's small procession finally arrived at the West Mountain Inn, it was greeted by dozens of professional and amateur photographers staking out the woods in hopes of at least one valuable shot of the soon-to-be-newlyweds. The tabloids had also set up a landing field on a nearby farm, where three helicopters were resting and men on cell phones scrambled to keep track of the wedding party.

But thanks to de Becker's thorough preparations, the wedding and reception went off pretty much without a hitch. The only photos taken that day were of Michael stepping out of a car wearing his baseball cap, and an aerial shot of the tent—hardly the stuff of a front-page exclusive.

Michael and Tracy arrive at an awards show in 1986. When the couple decided to get married, they were amazed at the lengths to which the tabloid newspapers went to cover the event.

So instead of a shot of the hassled couple, the tabloids ran stories of the elaborate—one paper called them "virtually paranoiac"—measures that de Becker and Michael had arranged to keep photographers and "his fans" at bay. Crestfallen admirers had waited as much as 10 hours to see their hero wed, *People* claimed, without mentioning that the actual number of admirers was much smaller than the number of photographers and media representatives.

The weekly magazine also reported that local residents near the inn were provided with red plastic wristbands to get through security checkpoints, and several others were threatened with arrest for simply "walking in the woods" near the inn. One nearby resident was quoted as saying, "I'm glad I'm not in show business. It all seems a bit crazy to me."

Michael resented the implication that he and Tracy had set out to deprive his fans of anything. "If you were to ask the average fan whether he or she would like to see a picture of our wedding, I'm sure most of them would say yes," he said. "But if you then asked if they thought it was okay for photographers to sneak through the woods, buzz the ceremony with helicopters, and bribe bartenders in order to get that picture, I have no doubt that the great majority would say, absolutely not!"

(Several years later, Michael would testify before a congressional committee in favor of a bill that would restrain just how far *paparazzi* could go to photograph the rich and famous. "I strongly disagree with those who would argue that some sort of Faustian bargain [an arrangement in which values are sacrificed for gain] has been struck whereby public figures are game, any time, any place, including within the confines of their own homes," he told the lawmakers. Needless to say, journalism groups across America opposed the legislation just as vehemently.)

People may not have gotten a choice wedding photo, but it nonetheless noted the arriving celebrities as if reading from a guest list: among them *Cheers* star Woody Harrelson, *Family Ties* costar Justine Bateman, and actors Dennis Quaid and Meg Ryan. It even reported the wedding nuptials precisely, noting that Tracy and Michael took their places in the closed-tent ceremony at "6:11 P.M." And, pointing out that inquiring helicopters nearly drowned out "the voices of the wedding party," *People* later asked the minister performing the ceremony if the racket rattled the couple. "[Michael] said not at all," replied the Reverend Joan O'Gorman, a mininster from Vermont who performed the ceremony. "Having just come from the set of *Casualties of War*, he scarcely notices helicopter noise anymore."

The hounding press even tracked the new Mr. and Mrs. Michael J. Fox on their honeymoon to the Caribbean island of Anguilla, where one photograher sat on a boat night and day with his powerful zoom-lens camera fixed on their hotel villa. Hotel security also caught two photographers hiding in the shrubs outside the couple's room at 3 A.M.

Michael and Tracy then sought refuge at her parents' beach house on Martha's Vineyard off Cape Cod, Massachusetts, a favorite summer playground for celebrities. There one particularly industrious *paparazzo* finally caught up with the newlyweds, managing to capture them in their swimsuits while he bobbed up offshore in a scuba outfit.

But Michael had already given the *paparazzi* a taste of their own medicine on Martha's Vineyard. Several days earlier, he and his wife were driving to the Pollans' home when two men—one eagerly snapping pictures—met them as the couple pulled up the drive. Frustrated, Michael picked up his own camera and began taking pictures of them. To his surprise, the two men fled. He trailed them by car five miles to a public phone booth, where they presumably tried to contact their employer. Now feeling cocky, Michael jumped out of his car and again began snapping pictures of the pair. To his astonishment, the startled photographer and his companion ran away seeking refuge in some shrubs.

"I have to admit," Michael said, "it felt great."

Michael takes a walk with his young son, Sam. By the late 1980s and early 1990s, he was devoting more time to his family and less to his career.

8

HAPPY DAYS

A YEAR AND A HALF after his wedding, things were going so well in Michael's acting career and family life that, at age 29, he often got the urge to pinch himself to see if he was dreaming it all. For starters, he had deals with Paramount studios for future movie projects, had agreed to direct a movie for entertainment titan Steven Spielberg, and owned a comfortable home in California and the rolling Vermont farm. Moreover, his megahit movie a few years back had spawned almost sure-fire successors—*Back to the Future* II and III. The icing on the cake was that he was also happily married, and the proud father of a child, his son Sam (who, with his name, everybody thought was going to be a studio mogul, Michael joked in a *GQ* magazine interview).

Wife Tracy said her husband was mellowing; he had given up smoking (one of his worst habits, and one he could never drop for long) and drinking backstage at rock concerts, and had furnished their Laurel Canyon house in a family way rather than bachelor fashion. In short, he was becoming a grown-up. Michael fully intended to start taking time from his hectic work schedule to be with his family—

especially now that his make-believe one, the entire cast of *Family Ties*, had finally gone their separate ways. After an amazing seven-year run, the show was ending. Michael and his on-camera father, actor Michael Gross, had seriously suggested the Keatons end the series by going down in a plane crash, so that there could be no Keaton reunions years later.

"The last year was tough, because Gary Goldberg, who was always the inspiration, was doing a film, and there was a little bit of the feeling that Gary had moved on," Michael told *GQ*. "But it was a credit to the writers that they could still pump it up every now and then—every three or four weeks there'd be a show where you'd think, This is fun again. And when we taped that last show, man, there were some serious waterworks."

The star of *Family Ties* knew the former hit show was the impetus for his success on television and the big screen. Apparently, however, the challenge of portraying a college-age young man—especially a go-getter who should've been raring to be out on his own but still lived with mom and dad—was becoming a bit difficult to pull off. "How can Alex be such an independent, intelligent, self-reliant human being and still live in the house and be arguing about who's talking on the phone?" Michael joked to *McCall's* magazine.

However grown-up Michael was becoming, his youthful good looks still allowed him to play characters 10 years younger. How else could he pull off high schooler Marty McFly in the *Back to the Future* sequels? *McCall's* suggested that one reason Michael still made a good living acting younger than his years was that his legions of fans—still mostly teenage girls—couldn't imagine their heartthrob coming of age. "Nobody will let him grow up," *Time* magazine also had noted. "He must remain harmless, asexual, a teen-dream doll or risk losing the devotion of his millions of chaperones."

Michael claimed not to be bothered by the younger-

looking-is-better theme to his life. "I've always looked young—and I enjoy it. If you can't be happy with who you are, you're in a lot of trouble."

By most accounts, Michael is happy with who he is. He has been universally described as boyishly handsome, yet he never lets those compliments go to his head. On the contrary, he makes jokes at his own expense—about his height, fame, and fortune. And to a person his acquaintances say he is a nice guy. "If I could think of something bad to tell you about Michael J. Fox, I would," movie producer Art Linson told *GQ*. "But I just can't. I wish I could make it more interesting for you, but, I mean, the slate's clean."

Linson produced an-out-of-character movie—*Casualties of War*—starring Michael and Sean Penn, who definitely doesn't have Fox's nice-guy reputation in Hollywood. In fact, in many ways the brooding young actor qualifies as a "rebel without a cause." While the movie was right up Penn's dark alley, it was a new dramatic challenge for

The two sequels to Back to the Future, *in which Michael again teamed up with Christopher Lloyd, were both very successful.*

Michael, who plays a conscientious soldier trying to retain a shred of humanity while those around him are succumbing to violent instincts.

The film is based on an actual event during the Vietnam War, when a small squad of soldiers on a long-range mission kidnapped and brutalized a young South Vietnamese girl in revenge for the atrocities they had witnessed at the hands of the Viet Cong. It was actually shot on location in Thailand, where the actors had to cope with military-style training and a country so foreign they couldn't wait to be back in the United States as filming came to a close. Of the five men, only Fox's character—who's as green as the jungle he finds himself thrust into—appears to have a conscience, and the nerve to try and prevent his buddies from losing theirs.

Penn, on the other hand, is a tough-looking and tough-acting sergeant upon whom his patrol counts to lead them safely through the war. But when his ticket home from the fighting is delayed, he loses his leadership instincts and goes on the warpath.

Washington Post reviewer Hal Hinson had admiring words for Brian DePalma, who directed the powerful film, calling it "great in the ways that the best DePalma films have been great, but with something more—something like soul." He had equally high praise for Michael, who he said was "marvelous throughout the film, but especially here, when he is forced to stand his ground. By stages, we see the transformations in this optimistic kid; we watch him close down emotionally and grow disillusioned. Fox makes Eriksson's struggle to hold onto himself palpable; he makes us feel that his soul is caving in."

Another critic, Pauline Kael, gave Michael some of his most glowing reviews ever, saying, "To play a young American in Vietnam who's instinctively thoughtful and idealistic is excruciatingly difficult, yet Fox never lets the character come across as a prig."

Although the critics felt the movie was good, audi-

ences didn't react as enthusiastically. But as with all box-office stars, Michael's influence in the entertainment industry was not dimmed by an occasional dud. He was, after all, making $5 million per movie appearance (a big raise from the $250,000 he had earned for *Back to the Future*), and Universal Studios seemed happy to have him, even if he insisted on a four-month vacation before starting on his next project after Sam was born. In addition to the *Back to the Future* sequels, he had been signed to do a comedy entitled *The Hard Way* costarring James Woods, who, like Penn, had a reputation as a brilliant but difficult Hollywood personality.

The film's plot sounded like Michael's biography: his character would be a TV celebrity who made it big-time

Director Brian DePalma's gritty Vietnam War film Casualties of War *was a serious role for Michael, who is pictured here with costars Sean Penn (right) and Don Harvey (background). However, although his performance drew good reviews, the film did not do as well at the box office as his comedies did.*

by starring in light-hearted comedies. His big problem? Guilt over how easily he had achieved fame and fortune, guilt that he struggles to overcome by redeeming himself as a dramatic actor. Michael told *GQ*: "Actors take on roles for a lot of reasons, and you can read whatever you want into this one. I think I can have fun with it."

With fame comes power in Hollywood, and Michael was not above pulling a few strings if it meant more time with his family or ensuring a movie that he liked got made. His lawyer-agent, Peter Benedek, told *GQ*, "I think he's really a genteel, gentle, lovely man who's just getting comfortable with . . . I hate to use the word 'power,' but he's getting comfortable with what he can accomplish in the motion-picture-and-television business."

Michael, a movie mogul? Well, not in the traditional sense of Samuel Goldwyn, perhaps; but he did have aspirations to produce and direct movies, as many actors have. And he also had the studio's backing; Michael had formed his own company, Snowback Productions, to work on projects for Paramount Studios.

So how did he keep fame and power from going to his head? Tracy says it's not the struggle one might think. "It's funny, because Michael has this really cocky side to him, where he's just on top of the world and he knows every inch of the clout he has," she said in an interview. "And two seconds later, he's the most insecure person in the world and he thinks it's all over. I think he walks a really fine line between the two sides, and that's why he never really lets loose that cocky side. Deep down, he thinks he's just Joe Schmo, and he's afraid everyone's gonna find out."

Michael, who has admitted that he occasionally feels like "some bozo who won the lottery," maintained his modesty is not a put-on. "The downplaying and what some people might perceive as excessive humility and ingratiating gratitude, it's really, truly quite genuine. I mean, when someone who's been teaching for 20 years has a positive impact on countless classes of kids and pulls in twenty-eight grand a year, and I made twenty-eight grand just now, just talking to you . . . I mean, how can you say I earned that?"

"You can't think that the way I peer out of the sides of my eyes and raise this eyebrow a little bit and then wait three seconds and say a line, that that's worth me being loved, adored, cherished, given first preference in any situation and showered with everything I ever want. If I get that, great. But you can't expect it. *You can't expect it.*"

Michael looks ahead in a scene from 1991's Doc Hollywood. *While he was filming this movie, he first experienced the symptoms of Parkinson's disease.*

9

COMING OF AGE

ALTHOUGH MICHAEL'S CAREER was going strong, he was beginning to show signs of weariness with the pace of his work life. Making *Casualties of War* had taken a lot out of him. In an interview, he even hinted that the demands and sacrifices of a successful movie career may have become more than he was willing to make—especially now that he had a reason to go home after his day on the set ended. "I really like showing up and acting, but it's so much fun at the end of the day to put it away and go home that the future path of my career is the last thing I wanna think about," he told *GQ*. "I just feel like I've exorcised so much confusion out of my life that that's almost all I can ask for. My future doesn't extend past these three or four months I'm gonna have with Tracy and Sam."

Certainly Michael had earned a rest. He had been working hard for several years with little break in the action. "People have been saying for the last four years, 'You're a workaholic. You should slow down,'" he told *People* in December 1989 as *Back to the Future, Part II* was released (at the time he was still working on part III). "But I'm still fulfilling commitments I made five years ago when I was single, when I might as well have been working."

Although not normally a worrier, Michael could imagine all sorts of futures if he did put the brakes on his career: taking a break from his hectic pace and then coming back to work only to discover no one remembers who he is; continuing acting only to find his fans no longer care (a fate that's befallen more actors than one could imagine); or retiring to live as a gentleman farmer in Vermont with his family. All this, before turning 30.

Michael was beginning to sound like a disillusioned young man who was questioning whether he needed to climb every mountain—or prove he was a dramatic actor. Indeed, it appeared he was beginning to accept himself for what he was, a wildly successful entertainer whose marvelous sense of comic timing had made him a bankable star. Perhaps, he thought, that wasn't such a bad thing.

The truth was, even though he periodically received good reviews for dramatic roles like he played in *Casualties of War*, his fans never seemed to appreciate his efforts as much as movie critics. The film wasn't a flop by any means, but neither was it a hit in the vein of *The Secret of My Success* or as popular as any of the *Back to the Future* trilogy. Michael even admitted that his own mother, Phyllis, wasn't as fond of *Casualties* as of his other movies. Nevertheless, he didn't apologize for stepping out of his comic character on occasion.

"I know that, in dramas, I haven't gotten much more than a deafening silence from people," he told *TV Guide*. "But I've had to try them for me. Dramas challenge me. I guess you could say I did these films because I didn't want to get pigeonholed in comedies."

Tired though he may have sounded in 1989, Michael's performance in *The Hard Way* was anything but worn-out, at least in critic Roger Ebert's opinion. "You have to listen really fast during this movie, but what you get is an earful of James Woods in full flower, and Michael J. Fox

so hyper he ventilates."

Woods, who made a dramatic career playing oddball, temperamental characters typically bucking authority, was no stranger to on-the-edge performances. He is about as un-calm an actor as there is. In *The Hard Way*, Woods plays a hardened New York cop who finds himself, under direct orders, babysitting Michael's character, Hollywood action star Nick Lang. Lang has decided to follow Woods (John Moss) every minute of the day to see how a real cop lives. While the plot line may seem tired, Ebert felt the performances were anything but, saying, "Woods and Fox seem to have agreed to crank up the voltage, to take the chance of playing every scene flat-out. They also take some chances with their images, or at least Fox does (Woods has always gloried in his role as a manic killer rat from speed city). The result is funny, fun, exciting, and, when you look beneath the glossy surface, an example of professionals who know their crafts and enjoy doing them well."

In action: Fox as a television star who wants to experience how real policemen live in The Hard Way.

However, Michael's role as an obsessed movie actor didn't translate into success at the box office for *The Hard Way*. This did not mean that he was losing his fans, however—just that they preferred to see him in comedic, rather than dramatic, roles. The comedy *Back to the Future II*, released the same year as *The Hard Way*, had not gotten very good reviews but it had brought in $120 million—an enviable earnings figure for any movie, let alone a sequel. At age 30, Michael realized that comedies were his bread and butter. "I guess, from the executives' point of view, comedy is safer for me, for them," he remarked. "People can see the money."

He returned with another lighthearted film in 1991. *Doc Hollywood* is the story of a hot-shot doctor who is on his way from Washington to Los Angeles to join a lucrative Beverly Hills practice as a plastic surgeon. It almost sounds like "Alex Keaton, M.D." except that in the movie Michael's character is even more lovable, because he has second thoughts about selling out his medical skills to make the rich and famous beautiful. He becomes sidetracked in Grady, South Carolina, after being arrested for crashing into a local magistrate's fence. To pay off his debt to society, Michael must work as a physician at the local small-town hospital.

Naturally, he'd rather be almost anywhere than this "Squash Capital of the South," but the one thing that keeps him from leaving—other than a court-imposed work-release sentence—is a beautiful, smart paramedic named Lou (Julie Warner). By the end of the film, Michael realizes there's more to life than making money, and that maybe being a small-town doctor isn't such a bad thing after all.

Roger Ebert called it a "sweetheart" of a movie, and this time audiences agreed; it earned a very respectable $65 million.

And yet, for the first time in his life Michael realized he didn't have an obvious goal in mind: being tall or a hockey player, making a living as an actor, or proving he could succeed despite all odds. His family had become more important than all these other quests, which at one point or another in his life had seemed all-consuming. "The answer is, I truly don't know what I want," he told *TV Guide* in 1991, shortly after completing *Doc Hollywood*. "I don't want to do a television series. I want to do dramas as well as comedies, but I have no idea what kind or in what order. Just give me the chance at them. Give me the chance at them. Give me the chance to be someone new occasionally. Alex Keaton, the Boy Prince—well, he can't stay with people forever. I'm sorry. He's grown up, he's gone, he's on his way to . . . whatever."

Michael, Tracy, and Sam at a 1999 awards show. Today, Michael is busy working on his hit television show Spin City; *because the show is filmed in New York, he can spend a lot of time with his family.*

10

TRUE GRIT

IT WAS DURING the filming of *Doc Hollywood* in Florida that Michael J. Fox first experienced the symptoms of Parkinson's disease. It started when his left pinkie began twitching. By the time he was accurately diagnosed, it was six months later and he was back in New York.

Michael chose to keep his illness secret for most of the 1990s, during which his career sputtered at times and it appeared he had either outgrown his fans or they'd outgrown him. No matter what kind of movie he made, none did terribly well. And time and again he seemed on the verge of retirement, or at least not taking this whole acting business as seriously as he once had.

Little did his fans know that he could probably see his life flashing before his eyes, although perhaps in slow motion. Parkinson's doesn't disable its victims overnight; the disease can take decades to slowly incapacitate people. Thus, Michael was struggling to come to terms with his illness in private, while valiantly trying to keep it from being splashed across tabloid pages until he decided it was time.

Meanwhile, his career reflected both his personal struggle and his

After a series of films that did poorly with critics and at the box office, Michael's supporting role in The American President *(1995) gave a boost to his flagging career.*

apparently waning box-office appeal at the same time. For instance, he had only two movies released in 1991, and none the following year. By 1993, however, he was working on four projects: *Where the Rivers Flow North*; *Life with Mikey*; *Homeward Bound: The Incredible Journey*; and *For Love or Money*. However, except for *Homeward Bound*, a delightful Disney movie where lost pets are the stars and actors speak their parts, none of these films was particularly well received. Michael was working, but most of his efforts through 1994 and 1995 were forgettable roles. "In the beginning of the '90s, things got real stale for me," he confessed to *US* magazine. "I sensed I was a franchise, and that's ultimately what got really old for me."

He took a break from work in 1994 (although he did

find time to finally earn his high school equivalency degree) and consciously avoided attending the usual ceremonies, events, and required appearances for an entertainer. Instead, he spent time with his growing family. In 1994 Tracy gave birth to twin daughters, Schuyler Frances and Acquinnah Kathleen, after Michael was reassured by his doctor that his condition was stable enough for him to raise other children. He and Tracy had both come from large families themselves. "I needed to live my life for my family and myself," Michael told *People*.

Although his career seemed to be floundering, what Michael did not do, he's said with satisfaction, is "panic." He no longer doubted his abilities. He was "a good actor," Michael told *TV Guide* several years later. "Not the world's greatest actor. And not the world's funniest actor. And not the world's greatest human being. Not the world's greatest father, or husband. But who can be any of that stuff? Who can be perfect? Not me."

In April 1995 Hollywood was speculating that Michael was being courted to star in another TV series by the end of the year. Rumor had it that he had been invited to return to the small screen several times over the years, but this time he might be seriously considering a break from feature-length movies.

For once, the rumors turned out to be true, although a bit premature. It wasn't until March 1996 that ABC announced it had committed to air 22 episodes of a series starring Michael and produced by Gary Goldberg, his old *Family Ties* mentor. Goldberg was now working for Dreamworks, a studio formed by entertainment giants Steven Spielberg, Jeffrey Katzenberg, and David Geffen.

What sparked Michael's return to the world of sitcoms? The actor suggested at one point that it was an emotional decision: part loneliness and part jealously. He had been filming *The Frighteners* for seven months on location halfway around the world in New Zealand when he began watching videotapes of popular American sitcoms to pass idle time. "My daughters had just been born and I was halfway around the world from my family. I was lonely," he told *TV Guide*. "People were sending me shows to entertain me. *Seinfeld*, *Friends*, *Ellen*, *The Larry Sanders Show*. I was watching this stuff, and thinking, 'Wow. . . . This is where things are happening.' And I thought, 'Can I still do that? Yeah. I can. That's what I do. And I want to do it again.'"

Another reason was family-related. Michael felt a return to television would allow him to work and live in New York City, where after an eight-hour day he could go to his permanent home to be with his wife and children.

Finding a suitable television series where he could have some creative input and work close to home were his priorities. Nevertheless, "I didn't tell my agent to put me into play," Michael insisted in an interview. "There's no financial impetus to do it. I set some ground rules: I have three young children and an East Coast–based lifestyle, so I said I want to shoot in New York. And I want to have some quality control."

At first Michael considered doing a series about a Canadian hockey player turned writer, but he decided not to after reading a sample script. Instead he settled on another show tentatively called *Spin*. Michael's character would—intentionally or not—resemble the supporting role he played in *The American President* as a close advisor to the commander in chief. Released in 1995, the movie starring Michael Douglas was called "one of the year's best films" by Roger Ebert.

Although Michael was named executive producer of the new show, he wanted its creators to realize up front that he couldn't guarantee his longevity, saying, "I said (Parkinson's) could get very bad or not get bad." Luckily, producer Jeffrey Katzenberg and ABC brass had no qualms about proceeding, and even built a new studio in New York just to film the show.

By September 1996, just as the fall television season

was getting under way, Michael was once again making the rounds on the publicity circuit plugging his latest project. Writer Chris Smith of the magazine *New York* was determined not to like Michael before one of the dozens of interviews he gave, but found himself warming up to the 35-year-old actor despite himself. He had expected to see an eminently "likable" Fox whom everyone has said looks far younger than his years. Instead, he was surprised to discover Michael not only looked his age, with visible wrinkles around his eyes, but at this point in his life, pretty much did and said whatever he felt, including chain-smoking cigarettes, a habit he had never kicked for long.

Michael got off on the right foot by admitting his last several films—including *For Love or Money*, *Life with Mikey*, *Greedy*, and *The Frighteners*—were bombs. And before long he retold the story of how his former lawyer and long-time agent, Peter Benedek, called to give him the overnight response to the showing of *Greedy*. "Mike, it's Pete," Fox recalled the brief conversation. "Sorry, man."

Michael recalled thinking that something had to change; he was tired of starring in films that for one reason or another weren't connecting with fans. So he hired a new agent, landed the smallish part in *The American President* (where he finally got good reviews), and then decided to embark on a return to television. When ABC offered him the role of Mike Flaherty, deputy to the hapless mayor of New York, he decided to jump back in with both feet as soon as he and Tracy read the pages of a sample script as it came over their fax machine. Both were laughing despite themselves.

Spin City, as the show came to be known, would give audiences an intimate view behind the scenes of New York's city hall, where the mayor's staffers struggle to put the best face on a boss whom they know is lucky to have his job. Michael's character, as much as he might deny it, resembles a grown-up Alex Keaton, one who usually knows just what to say or do—whether right or wrong—

In Spin City, *Michael plays a deputy mayor who must constantly get his boss (Barry Bostwick) out of sticky situations. The show has been very successful since it first aired in the fall of 1996, and Fox's performances netted him Golden Globe Awards in 1998 and 1999.*

to get his boss out of a jam. By all appearances, Michael had come full circle again, and seemed content to be there, in front of a live, studio audience that instantly responds to every head cock, smirk, or punch line he delivers.

As he began taping the first episode, "things started coming back to me," he told *US* magazine. "I realized I wasn't hungry and remembered I never ate before a show. Then I remembered how I'd go behind the curtain as the buzz of the audience started and get pumped. I remembered that I didn't feel prepared because you're never prepared. Because the audience comes in and brings you the rest of the show."

Michael was feeling right at home on the set of *Spin City*, which ABC had planted in the network's most desirable time slot: Tuesdays at 9:30 P.M., following its perennial hit *Home Improvement*. To no one's real surprise, the sexy new sitcom was a hit with Fox fans nationwide.

George Stephanopoulos, a former political advisor to President Bill Clinton, wrote a review of *Spin City* for *George*, a glossy magazine covering politics that was published by the late John F. Kennedy Jr. Stephanopoulos found it easy to relate to Mike Flaherty, he wrote, because they had three things in common: shortness, a thick head of hair, and an uncanny ability to put a "spin" on the latest crisis involving their bosses. "The show captures the way politics, in the age of the 24-hour news cycle, is often an exercise in crisis management: the way the best-laid plans are upended by an offhand comment tossed off while hopping into the car; the way the need for an extra hour of sleep is flushed away by the first rush of adrenaline after the radio blasts on in the morning; the way the pager is your constant companion, your lifeline and your worst enemy."

Michael was back in the saddle again, riding a familiar trail. "Once, I was so concerned about being tied down to one thing," he told *US.* "I wanted to try everything. Now I know nothing comes close to being as fun and fulfilling as this. It's 1996 and I'm still here, still making a good living and having a good time. When I was 20, I would have taken a bullet in the head to never have to be 35. Now I'm more comfortable and at peace with who I am. The greatest part of that is that I'm not the center of my life anymore—my family is."

He credits his wife Tracy for prodding him to take the role of Michael Flaherty in the first place. Calling her one of his "fiercest protectors," Michael said she gave him a loving lecture when he most needed it, telling him to "listen to your ears. Don't worry about taking roles because you think you have to be responsible. If you are taking a role because you are doing it for me (and the family), then that is silly. Ask yourself, is this funny?"

As she began reading the sample *Spin City* script as it peeled out of their fax, she knew instantly it was funny and told him: "You have to do this. You have to go back to TV." Michael took her advice and hasn't looked back since.

Entertainment Weekly sounded relieved that he had come back to televsision. "In another new TV season crowded with wooden stand-up comics learning how to act while starring in sitcoms, it is a blessed relief to see Michael J. Fox back on television," the magazine commented. "Fox plays Mike Flaherty, a hustling little bulldog of a deputy mayor of New York City, and the instant you see him, striding down an office hall, tossing out orders and sarcastic comments, you just relax. That's because you realize immediately you're in the hands of a pro—that Fox is one of those TV stars who can take even a lame joke and, through phrasing and timing, get a laugh out of you."

TV Guide was even more generous with its praise, saying, "Watching *Spin City*, it's apparent that no matter how good he may be in films, Fox is back where he belongs, in a sitcom." Just for kicks, it added, "Too bad he's Canadian and can't become a real politician here. For wouldn't it be wonderful to finally have a politician who's actually likable?"

So likable, in fact, that he has won two Golden Globe Awards as Best Lead Actor in a Comedy Series since *Spin City*'s first aired, and he has also been nominated for Emmys as well. And a year after *Spin City* debuted, Michael and Tracy were again a couple on television as well as in real life: she played one of Mike Flaherty's old girlfriends, meeting him on top of the Empire State Building on his birthday after promising to do so if both were unmarried at 30. However, things did not work out for the couple in the show: three of Flaherty's other former girlfriends also showed up.

Then, in October 1997, both Foxes graced the cover of

Architectural Digest, a decidedly grown-up magazine that features the homes of the rich and famous. After years of living in a stylish Los Angeles home, a New York apartment, and the Vermont farm, Michael and Tracy had bought a Fifth Avenue apartment to be—like other good parents—close to good neighborhoods and schools. "I'm grown up now, and it was time to have a grown-up place," Michael said.

Through it all, however, Michael has kept his illness hidden. But after suffering through the severe trembling fit while driving around the block at the 1998 Golden Globe

After the People *magazine article in which Michael and Tracy talked about his Parkinson's disease, Michael was interviewed by Barbara Walters on national television in December 1998. The actor told Walters that he has nothing but optimism for the future.*

Awards, he must have realized that his disease couldn't remain a secret much longer.

By spring 1998, he had completed the season's last episode of *Spin City* and was in what his neurologist described as the "late mild" stage of Parkinson's. (The disease progresses through three stages: mild, medium, and severe.) He decided to undergo surgery on his brain in the hopes that this procedure would alleviate the most violent trembling in his left arm. Although the four-hour operation, called a thalamotomy, is successful nine times out of ten, there was a small chance that Michael would end up paralyzed, or even die during the surgery. Michael reminded his surgeon that he had always been a risk-taker, starting with moving to the United States when he was 18 with no assurance he could make it as an actor. "The difference between what I did and what you're doing is that you know what you're doing," Michael told Dr. Cook.

The delicate operation, during which Michael was conscious but sedated, went off without a hitch, and his worst trembling disappeared. As for treating the remaining symptoms—occasional rigidity in his hips and trembling of the hands—a daily dose of medication called Sinemet is a big help.

Nonetheless, both Michael and his wife admit they were frightened at first by the initial diagnosis and still are some days. But they also knew that by supporting each other they could deal with the disease. Tracy told *People* that Michael's courage throughout the ordeal has been inspiring. "He's truly remarkable," she said. "I tend to worry about the future, and he's always saying to me, 'Why are you living through something that might happen?' He lives today. He lives the moment. And the moment is good."

On the *Spin City* set, Michael reluctantly was forced to scale back the more physical comedy and stunts he once did without a second thought (such as skateboarding and in-line skating). And he also had to limit how much time he could devote to daily rehearsals. "I can't do things a million times. I can only do them once or twice," he told *People*.

The response to the story about Michael's battle against Parkinson's has been remarkable. In a late December 1998 issue of *People*, half a dozen letters to the editor read more or less like this one from a California woman: "God bless you, Michael J. Fox. My mother had Parkinson's disease, and my cousin has it. Your courage to come forward and create a national discussion about the disease has given me and my family hope that Parkinson's will begin to receive the attention it desperately needs."

Commentators across America were supporting him as well. *Dallas Morning News* columnist Ed Bark wrote that Michael's disclosure "is cause to pause, reflect and then root hard for him." He got even more exposure during a highly watched interview with Barbara Walters on ABC's *20/20*. One of the main reasons Michael gave for being relatively calm about having Parkinson's was his sincere belief that medical science would have a cure for the condition by the time he was 50. He also credited his wife Tracy for supporting him from the first hint that something was wrong.

And when he received a second Golden Globe Award, for Best Actor in a Comedy Series, in January 1999, Michael gave a heartwarming speech that was met with a standing ovation. In it he thanked his family, friends, *Spin City* associates, and even his doctors, ending up with, "I just want to remind everybody. I'm sure you know this and don't need me to tell it to you, but we're so lucky to be able to do what we do, and just take every day and enjoy it. And enjoy doing what you're doing and enjoy being in this community. It's a tremendous gift. And I thank God for the gift that he gave me."

Moreover, like all individuals who have the strength and courage to face adversity head-on, Michael has an abundance of faith and an unshakable belief that his experience has made him a better, stronger person.

"The end is not pretty—I'd like to stop it from its logical conclusion—but I'm grateful," he said philosophically in the *People* interview. Moreover, combating his illness made him "a million times wiser. And more compassionate. I've realized I'm vulnerable, that no matter how many awards I'm given or how big my bank account is, I can be messed with like that. The end of the story is you die. We all die. So, accepting that, the issue becomes one of quality of life."

Thus, forced to face a mortality most people prefer to ignore, Michael chooses to live life as his parents taught him—one day at a time—and accept that life is not always fair. "The biggest thing is that I can be in this situation and still love life as much as I do," he says with amazement. "Life is great. Sometimes, though, you just have to put up with a little more crap."

CHRONOLOGY

1961   Michael Andrew Fox born on June 9 in Edmonton, Alberta, Canada

1976   Performs in *Leo and Me*, his first television series

1979   Appears in the television movie *Letters From Frank*; drops out of high school at age 18 and moves to Hollywood

1980   Appears in *Midnight Madness*, his first feature film

1982   Given the role of Alex P. Keaton in the sitcom *Family Ties*

1985   Plays the role of Marty McFly in *Back to the Future*; appears with Tracy Pollan on *Family Ties*; receives first Emmy nomination for *Family Ties*; *Teen Wolf* released

1986   Wins the Emmy as Best Lead Actor in a Comedy Series; stars in the film *Light of Day* with singer Joan Jett

1987   Wins second Emmy; *Family Ties* finishes the season as the second-highest rated show on television

1988   Marries actress Tracy Pollan privately in Vermont; wins his third Emmy for *Family Ties*; stars in *Bright Lights, Big City*

1989   *Family Ties* ceases production after seven years; son Samuel Michael Fox is born

1990   Father William Fox passes away

1991   Parkinson's disease diagnosed

1995   Twin daughters Aquinnah Kathleen Fox and Schuyler Frances Fox are born; coproduces the film *Coldblooded* and appears in a cameo role

1996   Critics and fans welcome debut of *Spin City*

1998   Reveals he has Parkinson's Disease in *People* magazine the day before Thanksgiving

1999   Wins second Golden Globe Award for *Spin City*; provides the voice for the mouse Stuart in the film *Stuart Little*

2000   Announces he will leave Spin City at the end of the 1999–2000 television season; Wins Emmy for Outstanding Lead Actor in a Comedy Series

2001   Started the *Michael J. Fox Foundation* to find a cure for Parkinson's Disease **www.michaeljfox.org**; Working on voice-overs for *Stuart Little 2, Disney's Atlantic:2001* and a film called *Interstate 60*

FILMOGRAPHY

Midnight Madness, 1980

Class of 1984, 1982

Back to the Future, 1985

Teen Wolf, 1985

Dear America, 1987 (voice)

Light of Day, 1987

The Secret of My Success, 1987

Bright Lights, Big City, 1988

Back to the Future, Part II, 1989

Casualties of War, 1989

Back to the Future, Part III, 1990

The Hard Way, 1991

Doc Hollywood, 1991

Homeward Bound: The Incredible Journey, 1993 (voice)

Life With Mikey, 1993

For Love or Money, 1993

Greedy, 1994

Where the Rivers Flow North, 1994

Coldblooded, 1995 (cameo)

Blue in the Face, 1995

The American President, 1995

Homeward Bound II: Lost in San Francisco, 1996 (voice)

The Frighteners, 1996

Mars Attacks!, 1996

Stuart Little, 1999 (voice)

APPENDIX

ORGANIZATIONS FOR PEOPLE WITH PARKINSON'S DISEASE

The Parkinson's Institute
1170 Morse Avenue
Sunnyvale, CA 94089
(408) 734-2800
1-800-786-2958

**American Parkinson's Disease
Association (APDA)**
1250 Hylan Boulevard, Suite 4B
Staten Island, NY 10305-1946
718-981-8001
1-800-223-2732

**Young Parkinson's Information
and Referral Center**
Glenbrook Hospital
2100 Pfingsten Road
Glenview, IL 60025
1-800-223-9776

**The Burnham Institute
(for biomedical research including
Parkinson's Disease)**
10901 North Torrey Pines Road
La Jolla, California 92037
(858) 646-3100

National Parkinson Foundation Inc.
Development Department
c/o Marc Lichtman or Lois Heffernan
1501 N.W. Ninth Avenue
Miami, FL 33136-1494
1-800-327-4545

Parkinson's Action Network
822 College Avenue, Ste. C.
Santa Rosa, CA 95404
(707) 544-1994
1-800-820-4716

**United Parkinson Foundation and the
International Tremor Foundation**
833 West Washington Boulevard
Chicago, IL 60607
(312) 733-1893

FURTHER READING

Daly, Marsha. *Michael J. Fox: On to the Future*. New York: St. Martin's Press, 1985.

Eichhorn, Dennis P. *Fox*. Seattle: Turman Publishing Co., 1987.

Greenberg, Keith Elliott. *Michael J. Fox*. Minneapolis: Lerner Publications Co., 1986.

Harmon, Dan. *Life Out of Focus: Alzheimer's Disease and Related Disorders*. Philadelphia: Chelsea House, 1999.

Kasbah, Mimi. *The Michael J. Fox Scrapbook*. New York: Random House, 1987.

INDEX

PICTURE CREDITS

RICHARD KOZAR is the author of Chelsea House biographies of Hillary Rodham Clinton and Elizabeth Dole. He lives in Latrobe, Pennsylvania, with his wife, Heidi, and daughters Caty and Macy.

JAMES SCOTT BRADY serves on the board of trustees with the Center to Prevent Handgun Violence and is the vice chairman of the Brain Injury Foundation. Mr. Brady served as assistant to the president and White House press secretary under President Ronald Reagan. He was severely injured in an assassination attempt on the president, but remained the White House press secretary until the end of the administration. Since leaving the White House, Mr. Brady has lobbied for stronger gun laws. In November 1993, President Bill Clinton signed the Brady Bill, a national law requiring a waiting period on handgun purchases and a background check on buyers.